DANCING with the SCARS 2

DANCING with the SCARS2

Out of Ashes Hope Arises

TJ Martini

First Printing September 2016

Layout and Design: Gary Lebeck;
Editing: Plus Two, Michelle Kaiser
Design Consultant: Mike Pieretti

How Do I Become a Christian; Pastor Bob Gunn

Photograph of TJ Martini: Jeff Spicer (jeffspicer.com)

Published Rivertree Media

Printed in the United States of America
10 9 8 7 6 5 4 3 2 1

Library of Congress Cataloging-in-Publication Data

Names: Martini, T. J., 1948- author.
Title: Dancing with the scars 2 / by TJ Martini.
Other titles: Dancing with the scars two
Description: Reno : Rivertree Media, 2016.
Identifiers: LCCN 2016037494 | ISBN 9780970501882 (pbk.)
Subjects: LCSH: Suffering--Religious aspects--Christianity. | Hope--Religious aspects--Christianity. | Consolation.
Classification: LCC BV4909 .M377 2016 | DDC 248.8/6--dc23 LC record available at https://lccn.loc.gov/2016037494

Dedication

To My Savior, My God:
Thank You, Father, for always showing me Your way and for the privilege of allowing me to do Your work here on earth.
I am honored to be Yours and so humble how
You are using me for Your purpose
and Your glory. I pray that You will continue to show
me how to help others to know who You are and what You can do
for them—no matter what they are going through.
May this book be their first step
toward a better life with You! I love You, Father God.
Thank You, for loving me first!

Table of Contents

There is an occasion for everything,and
a time for every activity under heaven:
a time to weep and a time to laugh;
a time to mourn and a time to dance
Ecclesiastes 3:1,4

"I assure you: You will weep and wail, but the
world will rejoice. You will become sorrowful,
but your sorrow will turn to joy."
John 16:20

Introduction

In this second volume of Dancing with the Scars, I am still in awe of how our God works through so many lives that were once in ruins without a hope in the world. Then the Holy Spirit takes hold and supernaturally brings them full circle into His light and for His glory. This, my friend, is grace—a true miracle from Heaven.

Many years ago, before I gave my life to Jesus, I used to think that Christians were so perfect—that they lived in some sort of a protective bubble and that nothing bad could ever happen to them. You can imagine my surprise when I found out how wrong I was!

The people in this book are real. Their stories are true. And every one of them is Christian—either prior to the challenges they faced or because of them. And I don't mean they just got religious. I mean they had or began an actual relationship with God, trusting in His will for them—at any cost—and then leaning on His strength during the absolute worst time in their lives.

I invite you to step into their world and read how these faithful few had to endure months—sometimes years—of devastation, heartache, and even life-threatening situations that literally brought them to their knees. Sometimes it was their choices that caused these unfavorable consequences. However, more often than not, many Christians will suffer hardships and tribulations—that are beyond their control—because they are Christians. "In the world you will have tribulation; but be of good cheer, I have overcome the world" (John 16:33).

For the ex madam of the world's most famous brothel or the Christian who fell from grace and robbed a bank; for the teen who would turn a normal day at school into a bloodbath or the homosexuals who spiraled downward because he/she could not escape his/her desires of the heart; for the addict who lost everything for one more high or the woman who ignored the desperate cries of a child, leaving her in the hands of a monster. Could they ever be forgiven? Could they ever forgive themselves?

These are just a few of the people you will meet inside this book, along with several others whose story is just as tragic and heartbreaking. They are all real victims of the world we live in—but they didn't stay victims for long. They are now victors for Christ and they want to share their story with you.

So, why then do Christians want to be Christians? If the road isn't easier and, all too often, even more difficult, why would anyone choose to be one? It's simple. Whether you are Christian or not, once we take our last breath in this life, it is NOT over! God made the human spirit to go on forever. The Bible (God's truth) promises that there is something much more beautiful and meaningful waiting for those who choose to follow Him! Christians know that if they surrender their lives to God and trust Him—no matter what tests they are put through here on earth—they will one day be with Him in Heaven for all eternity. And that, my friends, is a very long time!

Being Christian is not a religion—it is a lifestyle. It is people having a true and meaningful relationship with a God who they know is bigger and stronger than any challenge or heartache this life may bring.

What makes the Christian different isn't their perfection or righteousness. It is how they handle themselves in the worst of times, realizing they could not have made it without the guidance and love of a Savior.

Don't you think it's time you had a Savior? Don't you think everyone should? Whatever valley you are in, He will meet you there—and you will be able to "dance with the scars" for all eternity. Sounds like hope, doesn't it?

The Gates That Bind

This story will be difficult to tell as I relive the moments of a woman I barely recognize anymore. But knowing what I know now and what it took to get me here, would I change anything? I don't think I would. How I purposely chose to do the things I did is something I will never understand. On the other hand, I would not be who I am today had I not been who I was before.

My brother Roger and I were raised by our single mother who was divorced by the time I was three. My mother loved us and wanted the best for us, however, because she worked at night as a blackjack dealer, my brother and I were left to fend for ourselves most of the time. Roger and I were exposed to things we normally wouldn't have been exposed to had we had adult supervision. The parties we had at our house while our mom was gone subjected me to alcohol at a very early age.

By the time I was 12, I had smoked my first joint and was drinking alcoholic beverages several times a week. When I drank, I was uninhibited; it gave me a false sense of courage and strength. Unfortunately, while under the influence, I also made some really bad choices. It seemed the more "wrong" I would do while I was drinking, the more ashamed I would feel afterward, and I would drink even more to cover the pain. Then I would do something else that would make me feel even more ashamed and guilty, and drink again. I was in this cycle for years.

After a while, I started sneaking out at night to other parties with much older guys. When I drank too much, I would stay overnight because I was too afraid to go home drunk. The next day I would come home, but only after my mom had gone to work. One afternoon, after being out all night, Roger and I were at the house by ourselves. I had just gotten out of the shower and was drying my hair when my brother knocked on the bathroom door. "You have visitors," he announced. I wasn't expecting anyone, so I threw my robe on and peeked around the corner. I was surprised to see two uniformed policemen standing just inside the door.

After conversing with them for a minute, I found out that my mother had given my brother permission to call the police when I showed up at the house. Roger sat on the couch and pretended to watch TV while all this was going on. I was mortified. The officers told me that I was considered "incorrigible and a runaway" (because I had stayed out all night against my mother's wishes). These were considered grounds for them to handcuff me and take me away, which they did.

The next thing I knew, I was headed to juvenile hall. This was my first experience but, unfortunately, not my last. In fact, I spent many days in juvenile detention over the next five years for many different things; underage drinking, running away, burglary, curfew—to name a few. After awhile, I started to think of this correctional facility as my second home, and often liked it more than my own. At my mom's house, I had chores. I was the one who had to do the food shopping, and then push the cart full of groceries home. It was my job to make dinner as well as iron and clean. At the detention center, I was fed better and I didn't have to do anything to get it. The staff truly cared about me and I liked being there. They felt like family.

By the time I was 13, I was out of control. I was smoking cigarettes daily and my mom couldn't handle me anymore, so she sent me to live with my father in Fremont, California. This was the first time I had ever lived with him since they divorced ten years prior. I started school there and stayed with my father and his roommate in his friend's house.

Every morning I would walk to school and there would always be gang members and other delinquents congregating at the entrance. I had this sense of fear and often felt intimidated. I remembered thinking how different this school was than the ones I had attended in Nevada where it was friendly and more relaxed. A few weeks later, another man moved in with my dad and his friend. Now I was living there with three men.

My bedroom was the entire downstairs floor. It was secluded

and private and perfect for a teenager. Everyone else lived upstairs. One day I was in my room getting ready to go to my girlfriend's house. I had my foot up on the bed and was putting lotion on my leg when the man (who had just moved in) came into my room and approached me. He reached over and took the lotion out of my hands, and then asked if he could put some on me. I was so shocked and scared I don't even think I had sense enough to respond. The next thing I knew, he was rubbing my legs, and I freaked out! I couldn't believe that this 40 something-year-old man was doing this to me! When I saw my father later that day, I told him what his friend had done, but he didn't believe me. I think this hurt more than I wanted to admit.

I truly believed that my dad tried to be a good father, but he really didn't know how. I was so young when he left my mother, and now he had his own life; he had a steady girlfriend and they loved to party—then I showed up and put a halt to his freedom.

I didn't see much of my dad, even while living under the same roof, or maybe it was the other way around. He did not see me, even when I was right in front of him. I never got along with his girlfriend. I didn't like being in that house, especially after I was violated, so I started missing school—anything to keep me away from that house.

I hung around some friends who were as lost as I was and would indulge as much as I did—drinking, smoking and popping pills. Then I met an older man. I spent most my time with him at his house. I was 13, he was 32. I would hang out with him and his friends and would refuse to go home. Finally, my dad decided to intervene—attempting to care enough about me and be a real father. He told me I had to change my ways and my choice of friends, but I said "No!" I was unmanageable and unruly, so he sent me back to my mother, where I continued to rebel.

At 15, I had a brief stay with my grandfather. He was good to me, but I wasn't ready or willing to reciprocate. One night my cousin and I ended up getting into a huge fight after we had been drinking. I'm not even sure where my mom was at that point in my life, but after I fought with my cousin, I ran away. The detention center was not an option this time because I didn't want to be found. I ended up at a truck stop east of town. An old trucker picked me up and took me to the next truck stop, where I would hitch another ride.

I ended up riding with several more drivers across the country to the east coast. On my last ride, the driver pulled into the back of a truck stop where he and several other drivers pulled a "train"—one after another, taking full advantage of me—which was unsolicited and unapproved. In other words, I was gang raped. Afterwards, they got back in their trucks and drove away. I was left on the side of the road all alone and fifteen hundred miles from home. I was dazed and confused. I had been gone nearly ten months and, to this day, the ride home still isn't very clear, but I made it—eventually.

When I got back home, there was a warrant out for my arrest. My mom had boxed up all my belongings and left them at the juvenile detention center. The plan was to send me to Caliente (which was a prison for women under 18), but Paul, one of the staff members at the detention center, took pity on me and did his best to give me another option. I longed for a family and wanted the structure of a home life. I wasn't a bad kid. I just rebelled because there was no one who cared.

Paul went to his pastor and told him about me, and asked if there might be a family from the church who would want to be my foster parents. That weekend, the pastor announced this request to his congregation and a wonderful Christian couple stepped up and said, "Yes, we will!" They had never fostered a child before, but they were willing to give me a chance.

"Sharnel, these people want you. And right now you only have two choices. Caliente or this family," Paul explained with great compassion. "Which is it going to be?" Once I knew my choices, it didn't take me long to make the decision. "I choose the family." Paul was elated.

This couple was well-known at their church and in the community, and they treated me like their own daughter. Their home was an atmosphere of love. We actually prayed over our food every night—which I had never done before. I attended church regularly with them and their daughter (who was my age). This was where I first learned about God's love for me. A few weeks later, I accepted Jesus as my Lord and Savior but, unfortunately, I had no idea what I was saying or what I was doing. I just said the words without feeling anything inside. I think I did it more for this couple than for me, because I knew it would make them happy. I always loved God, from the time I was a little girl. I knew He was real. In fact, I used to want to be a nun, but it wasn't where my choices took me.

After a while, my foster parents told me that I needed to get a job, even if it was serving fast food. This was the turning point in our relationship. I knew I couldn't just live there indefinitely, but I couldn't see myself slinging food at McDonalds or Taco Bell either. So I found a job at the community college and took another job as a teller at a small local bank. I was 17 at the time and still going to high school. My day started at 5am. I didn't have a car so I took the bus to both jobs. This went on for several months until I turned 18. On my 18th birthday, I moved out and went back to live with my mom.

To this day I don't know why I left—these wonderful, loving people really cared about me and gave me the structured life I craved. They let me know what the real world would be like someday, and that I needed to be prepared to make my own way. Maybe it was just too structured and I wasn't used to it, and didn't want to be told what to do. They wanted me to go to college and have a normal healthy life, and I didn't feel worthy enough. So I rebelled.

I had these two roads laid out in front of me and the choice was mine to make—these solid caring people who wanted the best for me, or my mom who let me pick and choose how I wanted to live. I chose my mom. It seemed like the best road at the time. We were close and I loved her very much, even though she wasn't around to guide me into adulthood. We had a fairly good relationship outside of all the chaos, but I always knew what buttons to push in order to get my way with her—which I believe was why I chose that road instead. It was easier, for sure, at least in the beginning.

I was still working at the bank as a teller and it was during this time that I met one of the most powerful and influential men on the west coast, not for the "good" he had done, but more for the lifestyle he led. His name was Joe Conforte, owner of the most famous brothel in the world.

If you lived in this area long enough, you knew exactly where his brothel was—even before you knew what it was—and it was often the first thing you were asked about when you said you were from these parts. Signs and advertisements were displayed all over the city. Sometimes the brothel's name (alongside a risqué photo) was the first thing you would see at the airport when you got off a plane. And when you walked outside, there atop every taxicab, was an advertisement with directions to your "dream" destination. Yes, the world famous Mustang Ranch was indeed world famous as was its extravagant owner Joe Conforte.

A girlfriend of mine introduced me to Joe. Sandra arranged for us to have dinner with him at a very elite dinner house downtown—just the three of us. I remember feeling excited by all the attention Joe was getting. I was rather taken with the expensive car, the large amount money he carried around (which I noticed when he paid for dinner), his 10 carat diamond ring, and the costly Italian suit he wore.

We dined on exquisite food and expensive wine. After dinner, he drove us out to his "Ranch" in his Mercedes. When I say Ranch, I don't mean cows, sheep, horses and pastures. I mean prostitutes and pornography. Talk about another world. I had heard of this place before and the man who owned it, and I remember as a young teen seeing (off in the distance) this strand of colorful lights from the top of the freeway east of town. I used to call it "Candyland". However, this was a whole new experience being there inside and in person. And I was actually there with the "man" himself.

Sandra and I accompanied Joe as he drove us through the chain linked gate that opened with a click of a button, through the back entrance, and away from the action of the brothel itself. Suddenly, I found myself sitting in this huge private suite with the most eccentric and vagarious human being I had even met. The room was clean and colorful and had beautiful furniture and exquisite décor. There was also a bidet in the bathroom (which I had never seen before).

Joe got comfortable in his chair and lit his expensive cigar. Then he picked up the phone and ordered us all a bottle of wine. Next he called the cashier and asked for a few of his favorite "working girls" to come join us. When the girls came in, I was horrified at how little they wore. But Joe seemed to be enjoying every moment, slapping their bottoms and making them giggle. However, their prancing around in their nearly nakedness made me extremely uncomfortable. I was shocked, as some of them looked younger than me. But they were so proud. I soon realized that these girls weren't there in the room with us to "work"; he just liked having them around and showing them off like they were his prized possessions. At that time, it was still the three of us and, of course, the girls who just walked around looking cute. Before long, the room began to reek of cigar smoke and cheap perfume.

After a while, Joe shooed the girls away and called in the floor maid. He asked her to take Sandra to another room for the night so that she could sleep, and I was left there alone with him in this exotic suite. I was nervous and wasn't sure what he expected. After a few more glasses of wine I ended up staying and "things" happened. I wanted to say 'no', but I wasn't quite sure how, yet there was another side of me that just didn't care. Nonetheless, I didn't sleep much either. I kept thinking, "What am I doing here? Where's Sandra? How am I going to get out of this place?"

The next morning, I found out that Sandra had left. She never even spent the night. I was there all by myself with a floor maid, a bartender, a bodyguard, 40 hookers and their "pimp". I was ready to bolt, but for reasons I cannot explain, I stayed. Then I was driven home. This was the beginning of my 20-year relationship with Joe Conforte and how I eventually became the last madam of "The World Famous Mustang Ranch".

I spent many nights at the Ranch locked behind the gates that surrounded the compound. These gates were meant to either keep you in or keep you out—both being a form of restriction. In my case, and many others who lived a life similar to mine, the gates represented protection to keep the "unwelcome" out, which made us feel safe. But for others living within the gates, this kept them from leaving as well.

Over time, I became accustomed to the gates and to the man who built them. Joe was the originator of legal prostitution in Nevada. He was a Sicilian boy who, at the age of 12, came over from Italy on a boat to the east coast of the United States, and ran away to the west coast before he was 18. It was there that this young boy's desires and dreams all met as one.

While driving a taxi on the streets of San Francisco, he would pick up cab fares from men who were looking for women to entertain them. After a few months, Joe learned where every massage parlor, strip joint and underground escort and prostitution establishment was located. Whenever his customers would request this type of entertainment, he knew exactly where to take them.

It wasn't long before Joe realized that the majority of his fares were from men looking for alluring and stimulating recreation. Joe witnessed firsthand the large amounts of money that were transferring hands between his clients and these women—and all he was getting was cab fare! His business sense could see that this was big money and he decided it was time to venture out on his own and start his own business.

Joe moved to Nevada with two women and a television. Through many struggles with the law, Joe was persistent until prostitution became legalized, which led to many legal brothels all over the state of Nevada. However, none would ever have the status or the notoriety as "The World Famous Mustang Ranch".

My life had become even more dysfunctional as I continued working at the bank. Now, with this new connection with Joe, it seemed to have added another layer of craziness. He would often take me to dinner at pricey, classy restaurants and order the best vintage wine on the menu. The employees would go to the extreme to please their most recognizable customer. People would flock around him and he loved the attention. I was very impressed by it all. In the beginning, Joe would bring along a couple of his "working girls", and I continuously felt overdressed and out of place whenever they were around. But eventually I got used to them.

I was always paid well by Joe for my "services" rendered to him, and would go out to the Ranch to pick up my money. When I arrived, the floor maid would take me into a large kitchen area where a cook and several helpers would be working. It was amazing how well these "working girls" ate and how much they were catered to. There was a buffet of hot food from shrimp to prime rib, fresh vegetables, an array of desserts as well as a huge salad bar.

The floor maid sat me at Joe's special table and told me to wait until Joe could see me. I remembered feeling very uncomfortable while I waited to be called. The women there would walk past me, slowly giving me the once over, and some had the nerve to even question me. It was like I was new prey and they had to know who I was and what I was doing there.

A short time later, I jumped when the floor maid came back and announced, "Sharnel, Mr. Conforte will see you now." She led me back through a locked metal door that separated his area from the parlor—the parlor was where the ladies and customers would mingle. It was quite secure, and you couldn't get in unless the door was opened for you. I entered through a hallway, which made a sharp turn to the right. Behind the first door was a large suite and the door on the left was a large storage closet. The next door on the right was a Jacuzzi and a sauna; in front was an office. Through the last door there was an even larger suite which was Joe's private area. This was where I ended up. He didn't keep me waiting long.

When Joe walked in, I stood up and we hugged. Then he asked, "Do you need some change?", and then he handed me a $100.00 bill. Sometimes he would have me stay and eat dinner with him at the Ranch, and I would watch closely how the employees catered to him. His steak would always be cooked to perfection. "Send us a bottle of wine. Silver Oak," he would say.

During some of my visits, I would be intimate with him; other times I was not. I was never a paid prostitute, like the "working girls". I suppose I could have been, but I never felt right about it. I'm not sure what the difference is; what I was doing with Joe compared to what the "working girls" did at the Ranch—and maybe according to the world it was still prostitution—but I didn't feel like a prostitute. However, for me, I was Joe's girl (one of many) whenever he was in town, and what I did with him and for him was part of my role as his "mistress".

I felt God's hand was on my life through all of this. Not that He approved by any means, but it was like He allowed me to experience these things so that I could be that testimony later. He knew that someday it would all be for His glory and that He would turn all this evil into good one day. In Matthew 16:26 it says, "And what do you benefit if you gain the whole world but lose your own soul? Is anything worth more than your soul?"

Gain the world, lose my soul? I never knew this scripture until

I was saved, but in my heart it was exactly what I was feeling and why I didn't just become another "working girl"—a paid prostitute having sexual relations with anyone who came to the Ranch. I didn't want to lose my soul to gain the world. I didn't want to be that girl. I knew doing what I was doing with Joe wasn't right, but it didn't feel as wrong as the alternative either. Strange how we make up excuses and water down our reasons when it's our sin we are talking about.

During this time I was sharing an apartment with my mom. However, I was partying heavily and not fulfilling my responsibilities. I lost track of how many times I had been fired and rehired at the bank from missing work due to alcohol and drugs. My mom and I were supposed to split the bills but I was not living up to my end of the bargain. One night, she got drunk and moved all my things out on the porch and kicked me out of the house. I came home from my usual routine of partying, and was shocked to see all my belongings outside. I sobered up quickly and realized I had nowhere to go.

I called Joe and he came to my rescue. He moved me out to a tiny community called Lockwood, which was east of Reno—close to the Ranch but not on the actual property. There were about 25 rundown apartments that he owned, but only half a dozen of them were occupied. The place was horrible. I used to call it the Bates Motel. I couldn't complain because it was free. I had a place to live and I was very grateful, but I didn't have a job because I had just been fired again. I had no car, no income, and no food. Even if I had wanted a job there was no bus route that went out that far.

Lockwood was an area Joe had built with trailer homes and small houses. It became the place where the family of the Confortes lived along with several other Ranch employees. However, the apartments were so dilapidated that a friend of mine (who lived in the complex near me) had his roof literally drop into the middle of his living room during a snowstorm. Still, I felt blessed that I had a roof over my head and that it was intact.

This was about the time I started messing around with "crank" or "speed" (methamphetamines) and drinking even more. It's a wonder how I could pay for anything when I never had any money. But anyone who has ever experimented with drugs and/or alcohol knows that you would always find a way because you attracted people with the same desires as you. I knew exactly who had what I wanted, and I did whatever it took to get it.

Before I reached my 21st birthday, my life was spiraling out of control. Joe was in and out of the country, so I had to rely on my own ability to bring in the money I needed. I desperately wanted a change and to have a more steady income. This was when I found out that Joe needed someone to help take care of his wife, Sally; to be her caregiver and who would live in his house three days a week and care for her. I told Joe I wanted the job and he gave it to me. And so my new role began.

I was making great money, and Joe always paid me in cash, yet I had no idea what I was getting myself into. Living there with Sally three days a week in their beautiful house on the hill, I thought, "What could be the harm?" She needed me and I needed the money. I fed her, cleaned up after her, shopped and cooked, dispensed her meals, and bathed her. It was quite a job and Sally was not the easiest person to get along with. She liked her sheets ironed, her food cooked a certain way, and her grapes peeled. This woman was unrelenting and in a bad mood most of the time. Oh, the names people would call her behind her back! The more I got to know her, the more I understood why. That's when I swore I would never be like her.

Sally Burgess Conforte had had a very prominent life before Joe. She was married to what she called a "Jew in the Mafia" but it didn't last. She got her start in the brothel business soon after they divorced, but she was never a "working girl". It was in this business where she met Joe for the first time. She had owned two brothels in downtown Reno in the 50's. She and Joe were both considered small in the sex industry business. In those early days, in fact, they were each other's competition.

After meeting in eastern Nevada, they decided to merge and work together and become business partners. She would spend the next three decades of her life with Joe—building a multimillion dollar empire. Together Joe and Sally Conforte began one of the fastest growing businesses and would become well known around the world—Joe with his IRS issues and his public relations on TV and the news media, and Sally being his wife and business partner and who stood beside him through thick and thin.

Joe would give generously to churches, schools, and other charity organizations. He called himself a modern-day "Robin Hood" and always gave to the poor or less fortunate. But Sally was something else all together. She was demanding and always had to be right. Along with being bossy, meticulous, and rude, she could also be very mean and degrading.

As my relationship grew with Joe and the more he trusted me, he would say, "I never thought God would make two Sallys, but there are two of you!" I was appalled. I didn't want to be anything like her. Yes, I was strong-willed, loyal, faithful, and often mean if it suited my purpose, and even occasionally, I could be very rude. Sound familiar? Joe said where Sally and I mirrored each other most was when we "loved or cared about someone, no matter what they had done—lied, stole, cheated or murdered—you could always trust them and believe what they said, and you would always see the good."

Sally and Joe had a love/hate relationship, but they remained partners until she passed away. She was well aware of what he did with his "working girls", but she tried hard to deny it, or often just ignored it. Joe, however, was completely unaware of her "outside" activities until much later. Sally never knew about my relationship with Joe. I wouldn't have had the job as her caregiver if she had ever found out.

During the time I was taking care of Sally, I had a DUI pending and no valid driver's license, and she was determined to go visit her "boyfriend". She knew I wasn't supposed to be driving so she decided to get behind the wheel herself, even though she was legally blind! When that woman made up her mind to do something, she did it! She forced me to get into her Cadillac by threatening to take away my job, and I reluctantly obeyed. From the passenger's seat, I told her when to go right, left or straight. It was the most frightening experience of my life. I thought we were going to die.

From her house, we took a right out of the driveway and headed toward the traffic signal at the busy corner down the hill where we needed to turn left. I told Sally to get over to the far left, but she didn't know how far to go because she couldn't see. "More, Sally. Move all the way over into the left lane, about three more feet," I hollered, while holding on for dear life. She tried but she couldn't clearly distinguish anything in her path, and we ended up sideswiping three cars on the passenger side—my side. I screamed, she yelled. My heart was pounding.

The police came and it was a mess. Joe was out of the country when he got wind of it. He called me and started yelling, "Why were you letting her drive? And where in the hell were you going?" I didn't dare tell him the truth about her wanting to see her boyfriend, so I lied and told him Sally wanted to go shopping and she wouldn't take no for an answer. This must have satisfied him because he never brought it up again.

Sally was a very moody, miserable woman, but she became even more irritable whenever Joe would go out of the country. She would lash out at everyone around her. Unfortunately, I was often her target and nothing I did would make her happy. I wasn't sure how much more abuse I could take and I knew my employment would be coming to an end soon, so I asked Joe if there were any openings at the Ranch. He informed me that the only position open was for kitchen help at house number one. He didn't mention having me work on the floor as prostitute. Not that I wanted to, but still it surprised me. I wasn't sure if I should be offended because he thought I wasn't pretty enough, or that he planned to keep me for himself. I chose the latter and decided to accept the job even though it was one of the lowest paying jobs there. It was also extremely hard work because it was more tailored for a man.

The position was a dishwasher, but I wasn't just washing dishes. The job also included scrubbing large, heavy cast iron pans along with cleaning everything from the floor to walls, as well as three massive walk-in refrigerators. It was exhausting work, but the cook was kind enough to tip me for my efforts, which made me feel appreciated. I only held this job for a week before a cashier's position opened at house number two. I was relieved and accepted the new position immediately.

Thus began my career on the floor at the brothel. House number two was completely different from house number one. Not only was it smaller; it wasn't as busy. House number two was where the new girls started their working careers. Only the very special ones were assigned to house number one. Joe would monitor how they were booked; meaning how much money the girls would bring in according to how many customers would pick them (usually from a lineup or being requested ahead of time). House number two was also used for discipline whenever a girl messed up at house number one—stealing, drugs, fighting, etc. This kind of behavior was never tolerated and it greatly affected their income and living arrangements. House number one had the best living arrangements offered, including the best cooks and maids—and several other perks as well.

While I worked as a cashier, I learned many things about Joe and how the other employees treated him. Whenever they saw his Mercedes coming over the bridge, house number one would call house number two to let them know he was on his way. The cashiers would yell out to the employees and to the "working girls" that Joe was coming, and they would all rush around to make sure everything was in order. I was never quite sure if they did all this out of respect or out of fear. Perhaps it was a little of both.

After working as a cashier for about eight months, house number two closed for the winter because it wasn't making as much money as house number one. I found myself jobless once again and began drinking heavily and experimenting with "acid" and "mushrooms" (hallucinogenic drugs). The apartment complex where I lived in Lockwood was eventually condemned and once again I had no place to live.

I briefly moved in with a girlfriend who I had known since elementary school. My life became one big party. Drugs and alcohol flowed freely every day. I was a mess, both physically and emotionally. In between the parties, I would sober up just long enough to give thought to my life that wasn't going anywhere. Joe would call me from out of the country on occasion and would ask me how everything was going, and I would break down and sob. I told him all the crazy stuff I was doing, and then he would give me advice. He reminded me about his oldest son who lost his mind and was never the same again because of the drugs he had done—the very same ones I was doing.

"I want to stop, Joe, but I don't know how," I would often wail into the receiver. Although Joe offered to send for me several times, it never happened. Maybe it scared him too much because of what he went through with his son. Or maybe he didn't want the responsibility of my irresponsibility. Regardless of the reason, nothing changed. I stayed where I was, lost and confused, and knee-deep in my habit. Whenever I needed money, Joe would tell me to go to the Ranch and the money would be waiting at the cashier. And, of course, when I got the money, I would use it to buy my "party favors"—drugs and alcohol. My life was in a vicious cycle of destruction and heading nowhere fast.

In 1991, Joe became a fugitive of the United States because of tax evasion, racketeering, and money laundering—just to name a few. He was not allowed back into the country unless he chose to deal with the charges and do his time in prison. Joe would never go to prison so he stayed far away, often staying several months at a time in different countries—until his visa ran out.

During this time, my alcohol and drug use escalated. Joe called and said he was going to fly me to Rio De Janeiro, Brazil. This time he followed through. On December 24, 1991, I made my way to Brazil via San Francisco (so that I could get my visa). Joe had arranged for me to stay with some friends of his while I was there in San Francisco. They made sure I was safe and well cared for. I stayed with them over the holidays and through the New Year and left shortly after.

When I arrived in Brazil, I was completely mesmerized by my surroundings; the beauty, the living conditions and, of course, the obvious wealth. Joe had a penthouse at the beach, on the 21st floor. The upstairs portion of the house had a pool, Jacuzzi, sauna, and an area with a couch and big screen TV. Downstairs there were two large bedrooms and one small bedroom, three bathrooms, a large dining area, and two different entertainment areas. Through the kitchen was a small area with two bedrooms the size of walk-in closets for the three maids who lived on the premises. They slept in bunk beds. It was a family of three, two daughters and a mother; the mother was Joe's head maid.

I had my own bedroom by choice. In the mornings, Joe would come in and wake me in his usual stern manner, "Get up, Sharnel. Let's go! It's time!" And I would jump at his command. My body was still detoxifying and I had jet lag for several days following my arrival. Nonetheless, I would do as he asked, whenever he asked, or commanded. There were many things I wanted to do and see, but never could because Joe had other things he wanted to do, and because he said so, I obeyed. I was at his disposal, like it or not. I often had to remind myself that it was far better than what I had left behind. So I learned to be very grateful.

The language throughout Brazil is predominately Portuguese and Joe spoke it fluently, as well as Italian and Spanish. I didn't have any idea how to speak it or understand it and I would become very frustrated when trying to communicate with the maids, or anyone else for that matter. However, the longer I was there, the better I understood and could converse, even if I was often using sign language.

Rio was beautiful. The air was humid and hot. The beaches were full of tourists and locals. When I left Reno it was winter and very cold. But in Rio, it was their summer. Both sides of the penthouse had windows and sliding glass doors that led out to a veranda. The view was amazing. I would walk out on the veranda and see the crowded beaches and the ocean, and I could even hear the waves as they hit the shoreline.

I would sit for hours watching the hang gliders up in the mountains as they soared high into the air, and then gradually float to the ground. From the dining area, there was a mirror that covered one entire wall from floor to ceiling. On occasion, I would sit there so that I could see the water in the reflection. It was breathtaking.

In the early morning hours, I would enjoy the sights from the veranda, while Joe would sit in his chair, reading the Brazilian newspaper and smoking a cigar. He was as catered to in Rio as he was at the Ranch—with the maids running around serving him fresh-squeezed orange juice or cacao water with a straw. After Joe would finish reading his newspaper, he and I would go to the beach and walk or jog for several miles. Afterward, we would go to the cabana and get a fresh cacao, and then head back upstairs to have breakfast—pancakes were a favorite as they were out of this world—and he always had fresh smoked salmon and beluga caviar. While our breakfast was being prepared for us, we would start with fresh fruit, usually papaya or mango. This was our morning routine, just Joe and I together, and we usually sat in silence. He was engrossed in his readings and I was too intimidated to say much of anything, thinking it wouldn't be important to him anyway.

Eventually we learned to communicate and I found his conversations fascinating and his workload exhilarating. There were times when he thought my input was significant as well, which made me feel important, even though he had the final say (at all times), and thought he was always right. Of course, there were the regular "working girls" that would stay at the house with us. He had even sent for some from the Ranch, sometimes as many as five. Eventually, Joe moved me into the big house on the property with my own maid, and kept the girls to himself. Whenever it was time for him to leave the country to settle more of his affairs, he would send the girls back home, but I would stay behind.

Then there were those times we would travel together. He took me to places I had only dreamed about; Italy, France, and Switzerland—to name a few. It was fast and exciting, but also very lonely at times. Joe always had business to take care of and I was often left alone in the suite or just hanging around the hotel—for weeks or sometimes months at a time. Although Joe never told me I couldn't see anyone else, I knew better than to take up with another man. But after months of his absence, and without his knowledge, I became involved with a few special men. However, I knew that I was putting their lives in jeopardy, if not my own. If Joe would have ever found out, he would have had them killed. I knew this because he had done it before. Joe was never convicted or even considered a suspect, but the man who did the shooting, died in prison while serving a life sentence for 1st degree murder. This happened way before I came into the picture. It was definitely something I would never forget.

Joe played different roles with me throughout my life; father, sugar daddy, best friend, boss, and, toward the end, a business partner. He trusted me with everything. Joe was 43 years my senior. I was his mistress until the day the Ranch closed. He was out of the country a great deal of the time, especially when he went into hiding for tax evasion. At times he would call and I would meet him in different countries, or sometimes I would go alone to handle his affairs and to try to keep him from being extradited to the United States. That was the reason we traveled to so many countries—to see which ones had the best protection for him as a fugitive and to see which ones wouldn't extradite him back to the US. We were in Cuba for six months. But it was in Brazil where he finally put up his roots.

Joe eventually had a child out of wedlock. Her name was Annabelle, and she was born in Brazil. He was 70 years old at the time. Joe finally had what he needed to remain in Brazil until his death and could never be extradited for any reason because of this child's birthright. Joe was finally a free man and would never be convicted of any wrong doings that he had done while living in America. Annabelle stayed with us in Brazil, but her mother (who was one of Joe's girls) went back to the States. She had no desire to be tied down to a child. However, for me, this child was pure joy. I took care of Annabelle for four wonderful years and loved her as my own.

When it came time for me to leave, it was the hardest thing I ever had to do—to walk away from Annabelle and leave her there with no mother at all. I cried so hard, it felt as if my heart and soul were crushed forever. Annabelle called out for me, "Mama!" as she clung to my legs. Oh, how my soul broke in two. But still I walked away. I had to. It was time to deal with the legalities at "The World Famous Mustang Ranch" and I couldn't do it from Brazil.

After holding several positions at the Ranch—dishwasher, cashier, floor manager, bartender, and madam, I took over as general manager in 1997. I was 29 years old. Even from Brazil, Joe knew everything that was going on, and he had others watching me like a hawk. After a while, Joe realized that I was a loyal friend, and that I could be trusted.

Two years later, I assisted the government in the closure of the Ranch in 1999. I know I was tough back then, but I had to be in that business or I would have been eaten alive. And I probably wasn't the nicest person to be around, but I know I always did right by Joe.

Sally's health continued to decline from her diabetes, and in July 1991, she was put into a nursing home. She died in September 1992, from kidney failure. She was 75. Joe never came back for her funeral. If he had, he would have been arrested on the spot.

In 1999, the government and the IRS took over the brothel and my job as Joe's general manager and madam was over. I tried to hold onto some of the keepsakes from the Ranch that I thought Joe would want to have, maybe even to start a museum one day, but that never happened. The IRS wanted the buildings burned down so that no one could open those doors again under an AKA (also known as). But instead another brothel owner from Vegas put his bid in and everything was sold. Piece by piece, the most famous brothel in the world was taken apart and then lifted by helicopter to another location seven miles farther out—where it sits today as the "new" Mustang Ranch.

Fast forward a few years. My identity was now gone. I was an empty shell of a woman without purpose or value, or so I believed. I had been stripped of a past I never wanted, but was drawn into it "like a moth to a flame". Life had taken its toll when I suffered a horrific car accident in 2002, and my body slowly began to deteriorate. I had lost everything. I had to sell my house and my possessions. I went from having chauffeurs to not even owning a car; from mansions to a studio apartment with no heat. I was completely bedridden due to the accident. I couldn't sit or stand because of the extreme pain and the only position that didn't hurt was lying on my left side.

I severed relationships with most everyone in my life and was completely alone, except for this one person who used to be a Christian but had given up and turned back to his old ways. He started dealing pot and I needed some for my pain, and he gave it to me for nothing. I had just gotten my Social Security disability approved and it would be just enough for the bare necessities. It was 2003.

This one night, I was alone, fully medicated on pain pills, lying on my good side in a tiny bed in my one room studio apartment. I turned on my 6-inch TV that sat on a shelf in a corner and lit a joint. It was about 11pm. I was flipping through the channels and ended up on this station with Smokey Robinson. He was familiar and I had always liked him so I decided to watch. I noticed immediately that there was this light about him that was so beautiful and it drew me in, so I watched and listened some more. I didn't know until later that it was Trinity Broadcasting Network, a Christian station.

I had heard Smokey Robinson and his testimony about cocaine, but there was something different about him and I was captivated. I hung onto his every word for the next half hour. At the end of the broadcast, I repeated the Salvation prayer with him, and I felt the Lord's presence immediately. I thought this happened to everyone, but later I learned that it didn't. Not every believer feels the Holy Spirit move so quickly and so assuredly. I thought, too, that every new believer grew as fast as I had grown, but that wasn't the case either.

God became so alive in me and so real that over the next three days, I threw out the wine and my stash of pot and even the pain pills, even though I was still in excruciating pain. Afterward, I stopped watching television and listening to the radio. I found an old Bible on one of my shelves and began soaking up His words for twelve hours a day. I could not get enough, and I knew that I was bedridden for that reason alone. His words came alive, and all I wanted was the Lord. This was my life every day for the next three months, 12 hours a day. I was on fire and completely absorbed in His word—so much so that I didn't even think about the pain. And eventually, the pain actually started to subside and became something I could tolerate.

The friend who had given me the pot had eventually become a boyfriend, and after I had accepted Jesus in my life, I asked him about his old church. "Remember that church you went to a few years ago? I need to go to that church," though I had no idea why. "Take me to that church you used to go to," I pleaded. I had never even been to the church before, so I knew it had to be God's leading. This man ended up taking me and we even went together for awhile. I wanted him to feel the way I was feeling, but he wasn't ready.

One night he was sitting on the couch in my studio and the room was so small that I could hear him rolling a joint. It felt so demonic and so wrong, and it was so loud in my ears. I looked over at him and said, "You can't do that in here anymore." Needless to say, he didn't stick around.

Thirty days later, I was in full service at the church, volunteering as a nursery school teacher, and then as a teacher in preschool, and eventually at the elementary school level. Ninety days after being saved, I was baptized. I just knew I was on my way to greatness because of all I was to Him and for Him. I went to Bible College and graduated in 2006, and grew even more in my walk with Jesus. Little did I know what lay ahead and how my faith would be tested beyond anything I could have ever imagined.

I had just started a nonprofit ministry, hoping to help women get out of the sex trafficking industry. I called it "Scarlet Covering".

I had actually started this ministry at my church, but over a few short months, it had grown into an organization for the entire community. There were several prominent, influential women on my Board (the First Lady of Nevada among them), and a Municipal Court Judge who I reported to every week on behalf of my clients. I worked with undercover policemen and rode around with them looking for prostitutes working the streets. When these girls were picked up, there was no other choice than for them to be arrested, jailed, fined and then, eventually, put back on the streets after they did their time. However, "Scarlet Covering" gave them another choice.

These "ladies of the evening" could either volunteer to come with me and let me be their advocate—going to court with them and helping them get off the street—or they could go to jail. Many opted not to take my offer and chose jail instead. But there were some who did take my offer. These lost souls were eager to give up the bondage of their sex trafficking life and get the help that "Scarlet Covering" could give them. There were dozens of girls that went through this six-month process and many gave up their life of prostitution thanks to "Scarlet Covering". I felt so blessed that this ministry was growing so quickly and helping so many.

In February 2010, "Scarlet Covering" put on a "friend raiser" (as we called it) at the Governor's Mansion which was a huge success. Shortly after, things took a turn and went about as far south as they could go—hell bound on a bobsled. It was that quick.

Two months later, there were three detectives at my door. When I saw them, it didn't dawn on me for one minute that I had done anything wrong. In my past life, I had detectives following me everywhere because of the things I would do for Joe. I also had the government following me to other countries because Joe was a fugitive and I was running his business. Back then, I would have never answered the door. But now I had nothing to hide. I was a child of God.

These detectives came to interview me and to ask me questions about a complaint they had received and they needed to investigate. So, for the next two hours I shared with them the story of my neighbor Larry and how I had become his power of attorney.

Larry was much older and he lived alone in the apartment across the courtyard from me. We had been neighbors for more than six years and, during this time, I had grown to care for him deeply. I kept an eye on him to make sure he didn't need anything and I know he appreciated it. Larry was a full blown alcoholic and because I had lost my mother to alcoholism a few years before (and I, too, had already been where he was going), I wanted to be there when he needed a friend.

Larry spent a lot of time in his front yard watering and cooking on his barbeque, so this one time, when I hadn't seen any movement for a few days, I grew concerned. I walked over and opened his door, and the smell inside his apartment nearly choked me. He was lying on his couch covered in urine and feces. Larry had fallen down after getting drunk several days before, and had broken his hip and couldn't move. He ended up in the hospital for over a week and I visited him often. It was during this time that he asked me to be his power of attorney so that his bills would be paid. I didn't think anything of it and was happy to help. Our landlord also wanted to do a remodel in his apartment because of the mess Larry had made inside. I assisted in this as well, so that the landlord could not take advantage of the costs.

After Larry was released from the hospital, I moved him into a skill facility for his rehabilitation. This was when he made me his medical power of attorney and I was able to deal with the insurance company for him. Larry had two sons, but they hadn't wanted anything to do with him for a long time, so he chose me as his guardian, caregiver and friend.

This entire ordeal with his hospital stay and rehab took over a month and a half, but finally he was going home to a brand new, beautifully cleaned, newly painted and decorated apartment. Larry had been sober the entire time—the longest he had ever gone without a drink. I had never seen him look so healthy, and he felt better than he had in years.

With Larry being clean and sober, and having a new purpose in life, I decided to drive to Arizona to visit my dad for Father's Day. I was gone two weeks and couldn't wait to get home to see how Larry was doing. But the minute I saw him laying on his couch, I knew something was terribly wrong.

When he turned on his side, I saw an empty bottle of vodka underneath the covers. Larry never drank vodka. I knew someone had brought this to him and Larry was too weak to say no. That was all it took. A few weeks later, I found my friend dead on his new couch, in his feces with an empty bottle of vodka on the floor.

The alcohol had killed him and his estranged sons blamed me. This was in November 2009.

The detectives informed me that I was being sued for $75,000 by Larry's sons who thought I mishandled or stole some of their father's money. I had receipts for every penny I ever spent on behalf of my friend. I never comingled any funds. I never took anything that wasn't mine. And I never once took advantage in my role as Larry's power of attorney. The detectives seemed satisfied and left a few hours later. In June 2010, I was arrested.

I had no idea what the charges were until after I was put in jail. Three felonies: Exploitation of an elderly person, abuse and neglect, and embezzlement and theft. I had no one to turn to. Joe was out of my life and I was too embarrassed to call my church. I had no money. And with these accusations, my "Scarlet Covering" ministry soon fell out of my control. It was the Holy Spirit who got me through this because my flesh wanted to die.

Never in my entire life, with all the bad choices that I had made and all the wrong that I had done, did I ever think I would be in jail for any felony, let alone three. But even in jail, I felt God's hands on me and I continued to share Him with those around me, telling them of His greatness. I praised Him because I knew that's what I was supposed to do, as the Apostle Paul had done all those times when he was imprisoned for doing nothing wrong.

After contacting dozens of bail bondsmen and being rejected by them all, I gave up. I left it in the hands of God and He did not disappoint. The evening of the ninth day behind bars, I was sitting at a table with several other women looking at the clock on the wall. Suddenly I heard a Voice inside me whisper, and I spoke the words out loud, "I am going to be released tomorrow night at 9:20." The ladies at the table thought I was crazy. I thought I was crazy. I had no idea why I said that except that I knew it was true.

The following evening at 9:19, I heard the phone ring at the desk. The next thing I heard was my name being called and telling me I was being released. It was 9:20. I found out later that one of the bail bondsmen I had called took pity on me and said he'd put up the money. I had no collateral, nothing to offer him as a guarantee, except my word. I shared this with my pastor after I was released and he gave this man a check for $1500 to cover my expenses. He did not want any recognition or praise, but I knew God had used him and this bail bondsman in my time of need. This is what my God does!

A few months later, I went to court and was found guilty by a jury of my peers. I wasn't at all surprised by the verdict. In fact, when I walked past my pastor and a few of the people from church who had come to support me, I yelled out, "Praise God," on my way to being booked. I knew He was still on the throne. I spent the next two and half years in prison. And even though I was completely innocent, I knew I was exactly where God needed me to be.

I spent my days sharing with other women in prison the love God has for us all. I had a Bible study every week and a dozen ladies would squeeze into my cell and sit on the floor while I sat on my bed and shared with them the Good news of God's word. We weren't supposed to have other inmates in our cells, but one of the Correctional Officers (CO) stood by and watched, so that nothing would go wrong, and we wouldn't be interrupted.

God blessed me in every way as I helped lead more than 150 women, and "one man", to His saving faith over those few years. I knew the number of women I had helped because I had them sign a scroll whenever they vowed to accept Jesus as their Savior, and I hung the scroll on the wall. The "one man" who signed his name was the CO who listened outside my cell every week, and who had known the Lord before but was reignited and his vows were renewed. He didn't sign his real name though for concern that there would be trouble. So instead he wrote "Batman". God knew who he was, and so did I.

Even though I knew I was innocent and would someday be exonerated, I did my time as the Lord had willed. On August 6, 2014, two and a half years after I went into prison, I was a free woman. Once again, I was exactly where God needed me to be. Thus began my new testimony as I share this story with you.

Today I am walking proof that people can and do change, because God forgives if we repent and ask Him. I will share my life story with anyone who will listen and many hearts have been stirred knowing that, if I can be forgiven for all that I have done, they can too.

Recently I reconnected with a man I had known in high school and who I had even dated briefly. He's a believer now, and after spending a few months together sharing in God's grace and love, David proposed. I have been single for 48 years, and today I have the hope of being married one day and fulfilling a lifelong dream.

My life is full but I am always open to God's will.

One day, when asking the Lord to use me and to send me where He wants me to do His work, you can imagine my surprise when He put on my heart to reach out to Joe. In the spring of 2015, I called Joe after not talking to him in 16 years, and I asked if I could come and visit. He sent me a ticket early that summer and I was on my way.

After a 16-year separation, I was finally able to go to Brazil again and visit him. My plan was to share the gospel and not leave until he accepted Christ as His Savior. When I arrived, it was my pure delight to see Annabelle still living there with him. She said she remembered me, but it took her a few weeks to warm up to me. Soon she was following me everywhere and I delighted in her once again. She's now 20 and hates living with Joe because he says mean things to her and she is so hungry to be loved. I tried my best to let her know that her dad loved her, but that he just didn't know how to show it. I told her how much I loved her too. I stayed for the entire summer and shared with her God's amazing grace.

Although I was not always welcomed by Joe, he accepted that I was there. He looked at me and he knew I wasn't the same—I wasn't who I used to be to him—and this confused him. At 90 years old he was healthy, but with obvious signs of dementia, yet he still had young "working girls" at his beck and call. Old habits are hard to break, I guess.

I tried often to share with him the Good News about Jesus, and sometimes I thought he might even be listening. I heard him say several times, "Praise God" or "God must have brought you here," and I was so encouraged. Then other times he got rebellious and told me to get out. If he saw me reading my Bible and he was in one of his moods, he would get angry and tell me to leave. I spent a lot of time in that same room with the floor to ceiling mirror reflecting the water. This time it was very surreal as I looked out over the waters through different eyes and saw God's creation everywhere.

I know I left many seeds in Brazil, for both Joe and Annabelle, but only God knows if they will be planted deep enough into the man many women had known as their pimp; and to the child I called my own and still love with all my heart. I pray for them every day. If it be Your will God, let them know You and love You "with all their hearts, all their souls, all their minds, and with all their strength" (Mark 12:30).

This story is His glory and I am honored to share it with you. The gates that once would bind me, bind me no more. I am free and I thank God every day for loving me enough to save me.

Wreckage to Redemption

I'm not very proud of the choices I've made as an adult or the wreckage these choices left behind while on my road of self-destruction. These choices were all self-inflicted and I am now paying the heavy price for each one. As I share my story with you, I will open doors that have rarely been opened, let alone walked through. However, these doors hold the key to understanding why I am who I am today.

My father is Joseph. My mother is Mary. We are from a town in the east, but that is where the biblical similarities end. My family is Irish Catholic. I was raised outside of Philadelphia. My mom had nine sons in twelve years, of which I was the oldest. At one time, six of us shared a room—two double beds, three boys in each. From the outside we looked like a typical large American family. However, inside our home was far from typical. In 1968, our family did a commercial for Maytag and our photograph was in Life Magazine, showing my father and mother standing in front of a Maytag washer with all nine of their boys, ranging from ages 14 (me) to age two. The picture portrayed a wholesome, average family, but as you know, pictures can be deceiving.

My parents had a rocky relationship from the very beginning—one in which yelling, cursing, and physical abuse took place on a continuous basis. My father's discipline was arbitrary; hit first, ask questions later. But for reasons only she knew, my mom loved my dad and would do anything for him. Her "man" was number one and she, in spite of nine kids, found time to keep herself in shape and to keep up with his demands that she "look good" for him, all while taking care of her blessed brood.

When my dad was at work, the scene inside our home was nothing out of the ordinary except for having nine boys running around. It was typical chaos with splashes of love and laughter. As it grew closer to late afternoon, the mood inside our house would change dramatically. Inside the walls became a pressure cooker of tension as we all would anticipate my dad coming through the door, not knowing which "dad" would show up. More often than not, it was the angry, fierce father who would arrive. My brothers and I walked on eggshells and did whatever we could to stay on his good side—which seldom worked. When he drank on weekends, it only escalated his fury.

Joe, Sr. was well liked among his friends and peers, but I was afraid of him. He was physically violent, even to the point of beating me until he was out of breath. His goals for me were set high; nothing I did was ever good enough and there was no room for excuse or error. I grew up fearing him more than loving him. I was both physically and emotionally abused during my life at home by this tyrant I called "Dad."

What went on behind the walls and doors of our home was never mentioned. If it happened in today's world, my father would surely have been arrested and thrown in jail for child abuse. His anger and violence was often aimed at me, probably because I was the oldest and he expected more from me, although my brothers were recipients as well. I tried very hard to please him, but I never could. I used to pray at night and ask God, "Why did You give me a dad who hates me? I love You, Lord, but I don't understand." It's something I have asked myself even today.

My father was a schoolteacher and the brightest guy I knew. He was a tough, street-wise man of genius intelligence. At the tender age of six, I started helping my dad with his newspaper business. His route consisted of 800 homes during the week, and on weekends he delivered to 1,000 families. Occasionally he would wake me up at midnight and his other two workers and I would fold and deliver papers until 5am. During the week we would make collections. I'd take one side of the street and he'd do the other. His route was in a rough part of town, but it never bothered him nor slowed the service for his customers.

Being physically abused was not something you ever get used to, but it was a way of life for me. One of the worst beatings my dad ever gave me was when I was seven years old. I went to a carnival and was supposed to meet him at his car by 7:00pm, but I was 15 minutes late. When we got home, he came at me. No explanation was asked or given. He had his belt in hand and he beat me with it until he was exhausted. I had welts and bruises all over my body. He never aimed. He just raised his hand and swung as hard as he could and the belt landed wherever it may. A short time later, it was as if it never happened and it was never mentioned again—by anyone.

My mom and brothers sometimes witnessed my beatings and the damage they caused, but they were too afraid to say anything or come to my defense for fear one of them would be next, which was often the case. I never saw my dad hit my mom, but I suspected it due to the way she reacted when he raised his voice or his hands. I believe her reaction came from knowing how it felt. Needless to say, everyone kept quiet and went about their business as usual.

Our parents never attended church, but we children were made to go every Sunday, like good Catholics would. However, I had zero knowledge of the Bible and no personal relationship with Jesus. My brothers and I went to catechism and the older boys in the neighborhood taught us how to lie in confession. No way would I ever tell that priest what I was really thinking and doing. I already knew it was wrong, and I didn't care. But I certainly didn't want God to know.

My father's father was an alcoholic and he abused my dad throughout his childhood. You'd think my father would have learned how not to treat his children, but all his father did was give my dad "permission" to abuse us by example. Nevertheless, my grandpa loved me. I was his favorite and he was always nice to me whenever I went to see him. I think my dad resented the relationship I had with his dad because his dad was never that nice to him. Maybe that was part of the reason why I was the brunt of my father's ongoing anger. As I learned later, "hurt people hurt people".

My dad was a teacher and his expectations for his sons were extremely high; he demanded and expected that we excel and get straight A's. And for the most part, I did get straight A's throughout my entire elementary and high school career. It came easily for me. In college I could get a 3.0 without any effort or studying whatsoever. When I applied myself, I got A's. But it was never good enough for my dad. He would always find fault and would never commend me on anything. In his eyes, improvement was always needed.

I was popular with my friends—particularly the girls. I learned how to be a people pleaser very early because I tried so hard to please my father and to fit in with others. It was important that people liked and accepted me.

Saturdays were chore days for all the boys in our house who were older than five. My brothers and I would stare out the window and watch all our neighborhood friends throwing the ball around and playing, while we would be stuck inside cleaning every room, including floors and all the walls (at least as high as we could reach). I usually had kitchen duty; doing dishes, wiping counters and scrubbing floors. When my father came in for inspection, he would always find something wrong and make me do it over again until he thought it was right. He never helped. He sat at the table and paid the bills. My dad was (for the most part) an absentee dad, but he was always there for discipline. We could count on that.

As children, my brothers and I worked summer jobs down at the seashore, doing everything from selling newspapers to working on the boardwalk. All of our money was immediately handed over to our dad, from which we were given a small allowance. He told us he was putting the money away for us for college. But, of course, that never happened. When I turned 18, I went to the bank to withdraw my portion of the money for college fees and discovered that my dad had cleaned out the account. The money was never intended for our college expenses, but was used instead to help pay for his PhD. I was so angry, but not at all surprised. Everything was always about him.

It's true that I was a classic people pleaser, yet I had no self-esteem whatsoever. No one would have ever guessed I was so insecure by looking at me, as I charmed and hustled my way through life. We moved a lot so I had to make friends quickly. My people-pleasing nature helped me make a lot of friends, the good ones and the not so good.

When I was 11, my parents hired a sixteen-year-old girl that would come in and "babysit" us boys. After a while, this "babysitter" started having me do sexual things to her. I didn't know what to think. She would get drunk and then have me give her baths, along with other sexually-related acts. I can still smell her scent. I knew it was wrong but it felt good. It actually nauseated me but I was popular with my friends when I told them what this girl had me doing to her and what she would do to me. It was disgusting, but exciting too. I was just a boy and had not even gone through puberty yet, so it was very confusing. This went on for more than a year. I heard later that she was diagnosed with being a nymphomaniac. I think my mother suspected, but I never told her until much later.

I went to five different schools between kindergarten and 8th grade. It was tough, especially when I would arrive on the scene with that many brothers in tow, but we made it work. School was an outlet for me and a safe place, for the most part. I became a leader in high school—academically, athletically, socially, and politically—and was well liked by the teachers. Mom was proud. Dad was never around.

It was during the 8th grade that we moved to Wildwood, New Jersey, where I had to complete the last five weeks of the school year. However, with my people pleasing attitude, I charmed my way in and made friends quickly. When I was in the 10th grade, my dad wanted to uproot us again to Arizona so that he could get his doctorate in psychology. But my mother put her foot down. There was no way she was going to allow him to displace us again, so she told him, "No, Joe, we are not going."

My mom hoped her husband would see things her way and what was best for their children, but he didn't. Soon thereafter he left and she stayed behind with all of us boys. We became her world. I was 14 when my parents separated; however, they did not divorce until I was 21. My mother did everything she could to support us. In fact, as she was mending her broken heart, she worked as a claim's examiner for the State of New Jersey and was a waitress on the side—still while raising nine boys alone.

On the outside, my father's absence didn't faze me in the slightest; he was rarely home anyway. The peace that was never present when he was around was finally ours to enjoy. Yet, I know deep down there was that little boy who still craved his father's approval and who never got over the anger his father caused, which unfortunately affected me greatly for most of my adult life.

I excelled in high school; in grades, sports, and with the girls. I was captain of the football and track team and set numerous records each year. This was also about the same time that I discovered liquor. I didn't just drink it. I devoured it. One night after consuming more than my share, I got into a fight with a friend, split my hand open, and vomited on my feet. A few hours later, when the liquor wore off, and with little thought to the destruction around me, I announced, "Let's do it again!" I was hooked. I had found a way to feel good about my life. Alcohol leveled the playing field and numbed the pain deep inside of me.

You'd think I would have learned from this incident, but then that would have meant I was thinking straight, which I wasn't. Instead, what I saw through my eyes was that "cool kids" drank, and I was desperate to fit in—to be one of them. It made me more popular. So I drank, even while I was in training for sports. I took my positions on football and track serious enough not to indulge on weekdays so that I could give it my best. But when the weekends came around, I was the first one with a drink in my hand and the last one to leave the party.

Then there was college, which I ended up paying for myself, as well as using some scholarships and grants. By this time, I had been introduced to pot. Every year was a blur of sex, weed, alcohol, and fun, fun, fun. I rarely attended class, but I still managed to get good grades. I spent all my time drinking, partying, and sleeping with women. I had no serious relationships. I was in it for me. When I got bored, I left. When it got tough, I ran. I didn't complete my degree at my original college.

However, five years later I completed my degree at another college while I was working as a salesperson for a Fortune 500 company. The company required it; I desired it. I regret not getting my degree in those first four years and becoming a teacher and coach, as I originally intended. My life might have been so different.

My summers were spent in Wildwood, on the beach as a lifeguard. It was my retreat. I worked on the "stands" for three years. Then I was moved up to lieutenant of my crew, which made me responsible for about 25 other lifeguards—scheduling them and making sure they showed up and were doing their jobs. Despite drinking and partying every night, I would still get up early to run, work out, and train for lifeguard competitions. I never missed a day's work in all that time.

For the entire summer, I would stay with my mom and younger brothers in our home in Wildwood. It had originally been a duplex, but with several younger boys still under her roof, she needed more space. It was then that she decided to do a remodel and make the structure into one big house with two separate kitchens, six bedrooms, and two living rooms. Many times I invited my lifeguard friends to come stay with Mom and me, as she loved having all of us around. During the week, the guys and I were on our own for dinner, but every Sunday my mother spent most of the day in the kitchen cooking a spaghetti dinner for her sons, along with a couple dozen lifeguards who soon became her family too.

In 1976, my last year at Trenton State, I continued drinking and having many one-night stands with a variety of women. One day, on our way to the pub in the Student Center, a friend and I were approached by a young man who was with a ministry called Campus Crusade for Christ. He asked if we had ever heard the Good news about Jesus Christ. I said, "No, but I think we are about to." For the next 20 minutes, while using the tract *The Four Spiritual Laws*, this young man told us about the love God has for us all and about His Son Jesus. For the first time in my life this "God thing" made sense, and my friend and I both prayed right then and there to receive Christ as our Lord and Savior.

For the next three days, I didn't drink or leave the house. I read the Bible and felt encouraged by His words. Unfortunately, I had no spiritual leaders to guide me, no one to disciple me or keep me accountable, and my walk with Christ did not extend much past my acceptance of Him. I always believed there was a God, and I knew with all certainty that He was in my life back then, but Jesus was never my Lord. I never surrendered fully and completely to

Him, and I had no desire to give up my ways, nor did I know how to do this on my own. This process of fully surrendering would take me another 35 years. After those three days, I went back to doing the exact same things I had done before I accepted Jesus. I continued my daily routine of sex and alcohol as I foolishly attempted to maintain the image I had worked so hard to gain. My life was a lie. I was still out of control.

I left Trenton State College without a degree and moved back home with my mom. For the next two years I bounced around doing odd jobs, including doing substitute teaching in the winter and lifeguarding in the summer. The one constant in my life was liquor, as I continued to drink on a daily basis.

In the summer of 1976, I met Rosemary. She was from Pittsburgh and I fell madly in love and moved to Pittsburgh to be with her. Pittsburgh was where I began my long career in sales. The one thing I noticed immediately about being in sales was that it always came with an expense account, which allowed me to drink for free whenever I wanted. This perk eventually caused my drinking to escalate even more.

In 1982, my brother introduced me to cocaine, which began a 28-year love affair with the drug. Because of my irresponsible behavior and living as if life were all about me, I lost my relationship with Rosemary whom I had intended to marry. She was a responsible adult; I was not, nor did I want to be. At this point my life was starting a serious descent.

My outgoing personality (especially when intoxicated with limitless alcohol and cocaine) landed me several good sales jobs as a top salesman. The money was good, and along with an expense account, they provided me with a company car. I ended up working for a variety of corporations. At one point, I even held part ownership in a thriving health club. I was making great money, but because of my drug habit, it was never enough. I was living the life—and slowly killing myself.

Eventually I learned how to freebase cocaine, which is a far better high but way more expensive and very dangerous. I didn't care. I needed more. This worked for a while. Even though my drinking continued to increase, as did my cocaine use, I continued to meet my sales goals and managed to get promotions as well as big bonuses. However, that money was barely enough to keep up with the outrageous cost of my drug habit. As a result, I kept sending out my résumé, interviewing, and getting better jobs, which caused me to move frequently.

I once took the time to count how many times I had moved over my life, and it was a staggering 60 times! I realized that I was trying to run away from myself, but I kept taking me with me—geographically speaking. I thought if I kept moving, I would be okay; I just had to start over and everything would be fine. But the problem was "self". As hard as I tried and as far as I could go, I could not run away from me!

In 1988, I met Stacey. After we were together for a couple years, the next step should naturally be marriage, right? Well, I thought so. So in 1990 we married. I was 36. She was 13 years my junior. Marriage did not change my life at all. It did, however, change Stacey's, but not in a good way. She was looking for security, a family, and a home with a backyard to watch her children grow, but because of my career and my chosen lifestyle, we were never in one place long enough. I totally dominated the relationship. I was mean. I raged, and she bore the brunt of it.

I treated my wife with total disrespect and took full advantage of her. I was a horrible husband; irresponsible, absent, and an adulterer. We solved our problems by screaming and fighting, usually ending with me going out to a bar and being gone for several days at a time. I was still heavy into drugs and gave no thought to sleeping with whomever I wanted.

Because of a football injury in 1989, I started taking prescription pain pills. By the time Stacey and I were married, I was hooked on the pain pills, and smoking crack, and drinking every day as well. I got so hooked on the pain pills that I stole a prescription pad from my doctor and wrote them out myself. I was going to every pharmacy in town until they started getting suspicious. Then I would drive two hours away after calling in the prescription using the doctor's DEA (Drug Enforcement Agency) number. There were a few of us that would take turns picking up the prescription.

This one time, when it came my turn again, I went into the pharmacy to get pick up my pills and two undercover cops where there to meet me. They had every intention of taking me to jail, but I asked them if I could call my doctor first who I knew would straighten this mess out. When he answered, I begged and pleaded with him not to rat me out. After a few minutes, he told the cops that it was his prescription and he told me to get into his office immediately. When I went to see him, I got quite the lashing. He never gave me another prescription, but I managed to put the pills in my wife's name and did this for several more years. I was such a scumbag.

I later found out that I caused two pharmacists to lose their jobs because of my actions. It never got any better. I just changed the way I did it. I tried to balance being two different people; the "family guy" who managed to hold down a job, and the "party guy" who drank and used drugs around the clock.

Stacey and I were married just over 11 years. We had three boys, and I totally failed them all. It was all about me. I would work, then party, then work, and party some more. I broke promises to her, especially in the area of my vows. My addiction to drugs and alcohol increased and grew worse, and they eventually became my mistress. I loved my boys, but you would have never guessed it by my behavior or by my choices. I was an openly affectionate dad. I never had a problem hugging them or showing any of them that I loved them. I remember being patient with them too, which was surprising because I was always high on something.

I never hit my children in anger. My style of discipline was to take things away or have discussions as to why they were being punished. I established healthy boundaries early on and held them to it. Although I was often absent in their lives, they still witnessed many enraged outbursts. Between work requirements and the need to fuel an ever-increasing and raging addiction, I began to ignore my children, which will always be the biggest and most heartbreaking regret of my life. I never saw them when they were young and I never see them now. They don't want anything to do with me, and I don't blame them. I never earned their trust, and they never felt my love. I have learned that my middle child is suffering from emotional issues and substance abuse. Sins of the father run deep.

When enough was enough, I agreed to try rehab. The first "secular" rehab I was admitted to was in 1997. I went to 12 secular rehab centers in all. None of them worked.

In 2002, I was in Florida with a client for my company's National Sales Meeting. My mom was living in Marco Island nearby. I had robbed everyone I knew, including my mother, in order to keep my drug habit going. I didn't care who I hurt or who I stole from. I just needed a fix. She was so fed up with me. All I cared about was getting high and or making money to get high. I had many people working under me, and I would hob-knob with the president of the Fortune 500 Company. I had a suite at the World Trade Center in Orlando, drinking Johnny Walker Blue at $400 a bottle, and having narcotics delivered to my room. Hootie and the Blow Fish were playing downstairs and Mayor Rudy Giuliani was our speaker. This was a big deal.

Earlier that day, I had talked to my mom and told her I would be over to see her that evening, but I was running very late as usual. While I was driving there, she told me not to come, so I turned around and went back to the hotel. The next day we agreed that I would come for lunch, during which time I admitted to her my drug use and about defaulting on a loan that she had cosigned. My mom was hurt, but not surprised. She told me she forgave me, which made me feel even worse. As I was leaving, I put my arms around her and held her close. But it was different. I could tell by the way she hugged me and by some of the things she said that this would be the last time I would see her. When I glanced over toward her bedroom door, I noticed the opened Bible on her bed, something she had not displayed for many years. Something was very wrong. But she never said a word, and I never asked. Four weeks later she was dead.

The next week, I stored all my belongings and turned my back on everything. I checked myself into a drug and alcohol rehab center in Lancaster, Pennsylvania. This time I was serious about quitting. I managed to stay for over 30 days with the help of a caring counselor and a renewed relationship with Jesus Christ. There were many victories and some serious losses during my rehab stay, including the death of my mother. I was also served divorce papers and custody documents informing me that my soon-to-be ex wife would have full custody of our three boys. I was also told that I had lost my job. My rock bottom seemed to have no end. If I was ever going to drink again, this would have been the time. I had every excuse in the world to indulge, but I stayed strong and sober—only by the grace of God.

Following my release, I moved into a halfway house in York, Pennsylvania, and became involved with a Bible-believing, Christ-centered church in which I was an active member. I was on fire for Jesus, sharing the Gospel to whoever would listen. I got serious about my health and started working out and lifting weights. After nine months of sobriety, people could see the change. But despite all the successes, I grew weak and went back to using drugs and alcohol, and my world crashed once again.

Over the next seven years, my life spiraled downward into areas I never thought I would go, doing things I never thought I would do. Not only did my drinking increase (to about a quart and a half of rum a day), but so did my drug use, to the point that I became an IV drug user. My daily diet was rum, crack cocaine, Oxycontin (Oxycodone) pain pills, and heroin, which I was shooting intravenously. I used every day and all night long; never eating and rarely sleeping. At this point, not only did I use the drugs but I began dealing them, too, in order to support my expensive $1000 a day habit.

By this time, I was living in a crack house, broke and high. I lost all my teeth, which was mortifying. I had such perfect teeth. Now they were gone. I looked like Popeye the Sailorman. What money I could muster, I bought drugs and had them delivered COD to my door. At one point, I didn't go outside for over a month. In addition to losing my teeth, I lost the vision in my right eye, lost 30 pounds, and my skin was literally hanging off of me. I was also jaundiced from the damage that was done to my liver and pancreas. I was a physical wreck. I dared not look in the mirror for fear of the person I would see. In fact, I don't think I even owned a mirror at the time. I would never let anyone see me in this state, not even me.

A friend of mine had sent me some pictures of my boys. When I opened the envelope and saw them looking back at me, my heart ached. They were so handsome and had grown so much since I had seen them last. I was so sad and embarrassed by who

I had become. Seeing them reminded me of what a failure I was. I decided that suicide was the best and only answer. Of course, it wasn't what I really wanted, so I called a friend and he talked me through it; he told me how much Jesus loves me. This friend suggested that I try a well known, well established "Christian" rehab center called the Colony of Mercy at America's Keswick located in Whiting, New Jersey.

The minute he said the name Jesus, I knew this was where I needed to be. It was so close, I could almost touch it. The problem was that I couldn't be assigned to a bed for at least three months because there were several people in line ahead of me. I knew I would never stay sober that long. I prayed a lot and told God that if He really wanted me there, then He would have to help me. Every night I fought hard not to indulge, and every night I failed. Every day I regretted using, but not enough to stop.

A few weeks later someone ahead of me on the list had overdosed and another person had disappeared. The list kept getting shorter. In less than three weeks, I had moved to the top of the list. However, I was informed that I had to stay sober for five days in order to be accepted. It was the hardest thing I ever had to do in my life, but I did it. Soon I was on my way to freedom, although I knew it was going to be a very long, hard road. I went from Courtier to Timex; Louis Vuitton luggage to Glad garbage bags. I left my designer golf clubs, most of my designer suits and clothes, and two cars in the garage; and I never once looked back.

On April 29, 2010, I arrived at the Colony of Mercy, feeling overwhelmed yet more than ready to take on this laborious task.

I had wandered in the wilderness as a carnal Christian for over 35 years, until I surrendered completely to Jesus Christ in 2010. I was fully onboard by 2011, but I still had one more roadblock to conquer, one more mountain to clear. My addiction to heroin, cocaine, alcohol, and any other prescription or non prescription drug was out of control. This was not going to be easy. I needed more than a recovery center. I needed 24-hour watch. I needed a Savior. The rest that happened could only be the hand of God.

I was committed to completing the program by trusting Jesus Christ for His work in my life. I knew He was the only one who could change me. The words to the song "I Have Decided to Follow Jesus" echoed in my head:

"The world behind me, the Cross before me; no turning back, no turning back."

During my stay there, my life was transformed. Christ took my heart and filleted it. As it lay open—vulnerable and exposed—His Words, His Truths, His Love made their way inside, plunging down into the deepest part of my soul, where no one had ever been before. I was introduced to Galatians 2:20 and knew that not only had Jesus Christ died FOR me, but that He lived IN me and THROUGH me. It was no longer I who lived, but Christ who lived in me. Unlike in 1976, at Trenton State when I prayed to receive Christ into my heart, this time I fully surrendered my life to Him. He was not only the center of my life but my Power source, and He changed me forever. All this time, the Hounds of Heaven had never let me go. When I shared my story with other men there, I led them to know Jesus too. I knew that if Christ could save a wreck like me, He could save anyone—from wreckage to redemption; my story, His glory.

I also discovered that recovery was relational, not only with Jesus Christ, but also with others. I learned to work with the other men in the Colony. They saw the real me. In doing so, I learned how to put others' needs above my own.

I completed the four-month program on time and entered into a second phase called Discipleship. After another four months, I was offered an internship in which I was able to work with the chaplains of the Colony and counseled men in the program. I actually shared an office with the man who had been my chaplain during my stay at the Colony. Through Christ all things are possible. While I was there, one of my assignments was to write my testimony. I called it "From Wreckage to Redemption."

After a year in recovery, I was finally clean. This was when I met Cherri, the love of my life, and the great granddaughter of the founder of Keswick. How ironic was that? I got new teeth, a new life and, after a year, a new wife. From the very beginning of our friendship, it was clear that there was something different about this relationship, in that it was founded on our relationship with God first and foremost. Although there was much opposition to our getting to know each other, God was using our talks to bring about healing in Cherri, who had gone through several difficult marriages, and in me, who had prayed for an opportunity to be a godly husband. In July 2011, despite the opportunity to take a staff position at the Colony of Mercy, I felt the leading of the Holy Spirit to leave Keswick and pursue a dating relationship with

Cherri, culminating in our getting married January 21, 2012. God has blessed me greatly.

I needed Christ. Not I, but Christ (Galatians 2:20) is how I live my life these days. I know that I have been totally forgiven and that I have a new past (2Corinthians 5:17). Though there are consequences to my past sins, I am a child of God, a prince of the Almighty. I have value because He sees me as valuable. I don't let the troubles of the moment hide the glory of His purpose. In my healing, I am reaching for His scars.

In November of 2011, Cherri and I traveled to Pigeon Forge, Tennessee, to attend the Grace Fellowship International Exchanged Life conference. We ended up staying for the Workshop and Counseling Institute, thanks to the GFI staff providing scholarship money for both of us. We had traveled there on the proverbial "shoestring" and would not have been able to afford the tuition otherwise. That week at GFI was very significant in our lives. We met many wonderful people, including the staff of GFI, and gained a mentor in Dr. John Woodward. John has had a profound impact in our lives and ministry. We began to understand the truths of the Exchanged Life message in a clearer way as well as understanding how to apply that message to counseling. I felt drawn to GFI and even announced to John that I was coming on staff (not really understanding how these things worked). John gulped slightly and then made some wise suggestions, including pursuing my Master's degree at Luther Rice University. LRU taught their Master's in Biblical Counseling based on the Exchanged Life counseling model used at Grace Fellowship. I began that Master's program in January 2012, the same week that Cherri and I got married.

In July 2011, I started experiencing severe abdominal pain, and was diagnosed with chronic calcified pancreatitis in November of that year. The doctor told me that the condition was caused by my alcohol consumption for so many years and that it would be progressive. I was also told that I had a much greater risk of pancreatic cancer. Being very optimistic by nature, I really didn't pay much attention to the diagnosis, especially since I was feeling relatively good.

In February 2012, I was at home in New Jersey studying for my classes when two police officers came to the door. I was shocked when they said they had a warrant for my arrest. The picture they had of me was one that had been taken in January of 2010, when I weighed 128 pounds and my skin was hanging off of me. The officers couldn't believe that I was the same person and asked what had happened to me. I gladly answered, "Jesus!" That led into a discussion regarding a paper they were working on comparing Freud's Id, Ego, and Superego theory with Jesus' Sermon on the Mount. They actually took the handcuffs off me in the station so that I could use my Bible to help them with their paper. No matter where I went, God was using me.

I ended up in the local jail and then was transferred to the Cape May County Jail for five nights, until Cherri found a lawyer and arranged for me to be released. During the time in jail, there were many opportunities to share the love of Jesus with those men, many of whom were in jail for drugs. Even though it was extremely difficult being in jail and away from my new bride during that time, eight of those men prayed and received Christ as their Savior and Lord. I knew then that I had been confined for God's purpose. I also realized that Divine appointments aren't always comfortable.

In early April 2012, I was asked to go on a Missions trip to Guatemala to teach pastors how to counsel those in addiction. Addiction is epidemic in Latin America but few pastors had any training in dealing with it. In order to go to Guatemala, I needed to get my passport renewed. Little did I know that renewing my passport would pull up an old warrant that I had been told was taken care of.

In the summer of 2012, I began to experience an increased amount of abdominal pain. I refused to go to the hospital because I was into my second semester of school and had a major paper due. Finally, the pain became excruciating enough that I agreed to go to the emergency room. I was diagnosed with acute pancreatitis and an enlarged gall bladder. After several days, my local gastroenterologist had me transferred to Cooper University Hospital in Camden, New Jersey, a major teaching hospital with a top-notch GI team. It was there through some additional testing that I was found to have totally obstructed pancreatic ducts and the enzymes were not able to be released through those ducts—essentially my pancreas was digesting itself. The pain was excruciating and relentless. I wasn't allowed to eat, as that would trigger the pancreas to produce more enzymes. Needless to say, my weight began to drop significantly.

The determination was made that my only hope to survive was to have a Whipple procedure, known in the medical field as the most comprehensive and difficult abdominal surgery in medicine today. Although we didn't know it at the time, every doctor involved with my case, did not expect me to survive the surgery. The prayer team at Keswick sent out a prayer request that reached every corner of the globe. The whole world was praying for my recovery. There is such great power in prayer and God graciously allowed me to survive, but it was one of the most horrific times of pain that I have ever known.

During my time in the hospital, I had the opportunity to "witness" (sharing the Gospel) to many people and invite them to pray to receive Jesus as their Savior and Lord. From the time I got sick in July, 2012, up to the present, 50 people have prayed that prayer. One of the more memorable ones was a man named Gil, who shared the bed next to me. He was brought in on a day when several of my friends had come to visit me. I was in pretty bad shape, so they all stood over my bed and prayed for me. The room wasn't quite big enough to hold them all, but they squeezed in and took up most of the room in the process. The attendants, who were trying to wheel Gil to his side of the room, had to wait in the hall until my friends were through praying for me. The look on Gil's face was so angry and hostile. His temper flared often and he would routinely throw things, while yelling and cursing at the doctors and nurses and ordering them out of the room.

One very early morning, Gil had a problem that needed immediate attention at the very same time that my fever had dangerously spiked due to a blood infection. Half a dozen doctors and nurses were in the room attending to both of us. After things had quieted down, I felt the Lord prompting me to talk to Gil. "Really, Lord? Now?" That was the last thing I wanted to do. But God tugged on me again, and I gave in.

"Gil," I said to him. "You have got to be the angriest one-legged Puerto Rican I have ever met. What are you so angry about?" He said, "Joe, I am the *only* one-legged Puerto Rican you have ever met!" I laughed and agreed, which lightened the mood.

In the ensuing conversation, Gil shared with me that he was angry because the doctors had amputated his leg without his permission (his wife had given permission for him instead), and he was afraid he was going to lose the other leg. Then I asked him, "But why were you so angry that day you were brought to our room?" Gil looked down and seemed hesitant at first. Then he replied, "Joe, I wasn't angry. I saw all of you praying and I wished I could have been a part of that group."

It was as if the Holy Spirit had pitched a softball straight at me. I took my cue and ran with it. I talked with Gil about the love Jesus had for him, and asked him if he would like to pray to receive Him. We prayed together that night and Gil came into the family of God. Gil's anger didn't vanish immediately, but it was clear that his heart had changed and I look forward to spending eternity with him.

Then there was Carol. I had been admitted to the hospital for a kidney issue and was complaining to Cherri about being there. She reminded me that I wasn't there for my kidney. I was there because someone needed to hear about Jesus. About that time we saw the surgeon who had done my Whipple procedure just leaving a patient's room. A few minutes later, we saw the patient exit the room to take a walk. Cherri and I caught up with her and introduced ourselves. Her name was Carol.

As we talked, I found out that Carol had been scheduled for a Whipple, but when they got inside, they found that she had pancreatic cancer everywhere in her abdomen. They closed her up without doing the rest of the surgery and informed her that she most likely only had a few weeks to live. Tears slid down her cheeks as she spoke. I felt God's tugging once again and knew with all certainty that this was not a chance meeting. I was able to talk with Carol about God and she prayed to receive Him as her Savior and Lord. Her countenance changed drastically. She went from devastated to delirious, and her tears this time were that of joy. I said to her that night, "Carol, you have gone from terminal to eternal." I know I will see this precious sister again one day.

I am humbled how God keeps using me for His purpose and Glory. I don't know how long this broken abused body of mine will hold out. It's often "touch and go" as I make my way back to the ER and fight for my life. Sometimes I think, "This is it, Lord. I'm coming Home." But then He gives me just enough strength to share His amazing truths with someone else. And after they accept His gift of salvation, God heals me and sends me home to my house, not His.

I'll bet there have been more times than I can count that God has sent me in an ambulance or riding next to my wife as she rushes through traffic to get me to the ER before I stop breathing. But there hasn't been one time that I have gone where there isn't someone I help bring to Jesus. Cherri and I both know that when I can't breathe and am fighting for my life, that it isn't really my life at all that I'm fighting for. It's those who God needs me to talk to when I get to the hospital.

My physical condition continues to be difficult. I deal with pain and fatigue on a daily basis. My pancreas is in the process of burning out. When it does, I will become a very brittle diabetic, along with the other issues of scar tissue, kidney problems, breathing problems, and vascular issues. We are blessed with a tremendous team of doctors who deeply care about my health and wellbeing. Cherri and I continuously minister to those suffering in addiction, and also to family members of those addicts. We are in full-time ministry, including my counseling at the Colony of Mercy on an as needed basis.

We are on missionary support as we watch God daily do what He does best: "Show Up and Show Off." He is the only reason that I am still alive, and though life is very difficult, it is a privilege to serve Him in any way that He sees fit. I will spend the rest of this life thanking Him and bringing others to the knowledge of Him, until I take my final breath. God uses me in the most peculiar ways, sometimes on my deathbed (literally), but it's for His glory that I am able to speak so boldly, and because of where I've been, people listen. Plus, being on my deathbed, what have I got to lose? If they weren't saved, they're getting the Gospel; and if they were saved, they're getting the Gospel. It's a win win.

My God has truly taken me from wreckage to redemption and I am honored to serve Him in such a way as this. To God be the glory forever.

Amazing Grace

I was two years old when my parents were divorced. My father pretty much disappeared after that, and was gone for most of my childhood. He left behind three children: my sister, my brother, and me. A short time later, my mom married a man named Dennis. I found out that she had been having an affair with him even before she divorced my dad. This marriage produced two more children: a boy and a girl. Now there were five of us growing up in our house. I was the one in the middle.

During this period of my life, my mom did the best she could raising all of us, but because she worked so much we hardly ever saw her. My new stepdad rarely worked and never contributed in helping our family out financially. He usually spent most of his days in a casino, which meant my mom had to work two or sometimes even three jobs just to make ends meet. Those rare days when she was home, my mom was so consumed with pleasing her husband that she didn't have the time to give her children much attention or affection.

Although I didn't understand it at first, her way of showing us kids her love was by working hard to provide for us financially. That was it. When she came home, the "love" was over, although my longing for her was not. All I desperately wanted from her was a hug, a kiss, a shared conversation—just to know that she was interested in me—but not once did that ever happen.

My mom was miserable and irritable. In fact, I can't recall a time when she wasn't. She angered easily and when we upset her in the least, she would turn violent and hit us. Sadly, it was never just a normal spanking like a paddle on the bottom. We were whipped. Then she'd throw whatever was close—hangers, shoes, books—anything within reach to make her point. The energy she exerted seemed to scream out, "I hate my life and you are just making things worse, so stop it!" Unknowingly, my mother destroyed my self-esteem, and made me constantly question who I was, and what I was worth. She seemed determined to belittle me and break me down—and I lost my innocence in the process. Basically she made me feel unloved and worthless.

At mealtime we never sat at the table as a family. It was only us kids who sat together. My oldest sister, Nicole, was the one who would step up in my mother's absence and take over as our guardian making sure we all had something to eat. She was the one who kept us together as a family. The rare times when my mom was around, I panicked whenever I accidentally spilled something at the table or on the floor. It made her furious and she would lash out at me, screaming horrible things children should never hear from anyone—especially not from their mother.

Whenever things got this bad, we knew it was her breaking point. We also knew that our punishment was close—and it would be brutal. With wire coat hanger in hand, my mom would violently whip us wherever it landed as the hanger met our flesh. Often times she would make us stand and face the wall. Sometimes we would be holding books over our heads, which seemed to get heavier with each minute that passed, or just holding up our hands. If we lowered them she would whip us on the backs of our legs or cruelly pinch us, and then twist her nails into the tender part of our arms or legs. The pain was excruciating. The memory would last a lifetime.

I was around ten when my real dad came back into my life. We three older kids spent a week with him every other week, which made me feel like a living ping pong ball, bouncing back and forth between parents. During the "back and forth" process, I attended nine different schools in nine different areas. I never had a close girlfriend or any other long-term friendship for that matter. My siblings were the only friends I had at the time.

After a few years, I started feeling the strain of being unwanted and unloved even more, especially since my dad came back into my life. To me, it seemed the only reason he even wanted me around at all was so that he didn't have to pay my mom child support. He never acted like he cared about any of us. In fact, when we were with him, there were days when there wasn't very much to eat, so the responsibility of feeding and caring for my brother and I would once again fall on the young shoulders of my seventeen-year-old sister Nicole. Then it was back to my mom's house.

My stepdad hardly ever spoke to me. In fact, he rarely acknowledged my existence. Most of the time, he would go out of his way to let me know how much he disliked and resented me being there. I was starved for attention and affection, and at this point, it didn't matter where or who it came from. So when Kyle came into my life, I took notice. I was eager to please and so very ready to be loved. I was also just 13 years old. Kyle was 20. He was a friend of Nicole's boyfriend.

Desperate for any attention, I developed a huge crush on Kyle the more he came around. He knew it and he took advantage of it. He would get me down on the floor and playfully wrestle with me. Then he would cuddle as we lay there intertwined. His breathing was rapid and hard. I felt a rush of excitement whenever he held me, something I had been longing for my enter life. So this was what love felt like—warm, inviting, full of hope and promise. My heart leaped with joy. I never wanted it to end.

Not only was I young but I was also very naïve at the time. Kyle took advantage of this too. I was completely ignorant of foreplay and sex, so it was confusing to me when one afternoon Kyle pulled his pants off and forced my head into his lap. He guided me with his words and then showed me exactly what he wanted me to do. And because I wanted so much to please him, I obeyed. This act of submission seemed to satisfy him completely, so it pleased me as well. Although I still had no idea what I had done, I was willing to do whatever he desired, whenever he desired it, so that he would love me.

Before long he began sneaking into my room at night. This is when his fondling under my pajamas turned into rough and thoughtless caressing. I had never been treated with much tenderness in my life, so his advances and demands did not seem that unusual. I was an eager participant because of my constant need to be loved, and Kyle used my longing to satisfy his manly cravings. I was only a child, barely 13 years old, when I lost my virginity. I still had no idea what I was doing. But I felt loved at long last.

When I was 14, I got into a huge argument with my stepdad. I was acting out in typical rebellious fashion as teenagers often do, but I had no idea that the consequences of my actions would be so severe. My mom chose to take Dennis' side. A short time later, she threw me out of the house. I could not understand for the life of me why she would choose her husband over her child.

Out on the street I felt abandoned and alone. I was scared and lost as I bounced from house to house, friend to friend, family member to family member—staying anywhere I could with whoever would take me in, yet never a place to call home. I became so depressed. After a while I made a despairing attempt to commit suicide by swallowing a bottle of sleeping pills. I didn't do it for the attention, but out of sheer desperation. I felt helpless and hopeless. The hurt ran deep.

My sister Nicole was the one who found me in the bathtub. She revived me. Then I vomited repeatedly. Nicole drove me to a hospital where I was administered charcoal to soak up the poison. It was nasty and I continued to vomit even more—till there was nothing left inside.

Even though I had never really acknowledged God being in my life, I could truly feel His protection as He held me in His strong embrace. He never gave up on me. Nicole came to my rescue again when she let me stay with her while I recovered. Her concern for me was obvious and I was so grateful.

Word spread quickly among my family and friends, and soon everyone knew what I had done. My mom and my dad were completely indifferent. They never once acknowledged my actions or ever even talked to me about it. It was as if it never happened, making me feel all the more alone. Kyle was the only person in my life who comforted me through this emotional time and who made me feel as if I were truly loved. But all too soon his love became an obsession.

After I felt strong enough to leave my sister's care, I rented a room and got a part time job as a hostess at a restaurant while attending my high school classes. Soon I started noticing that whenever I would leave my house, Kyle would follow me. Everywhere I went he was there. During P.E., he would always watch me from across the street. At night, he would watch me through my windows. I discovered this when I noticed a pile of cigarette butts outside my bedroom window—the same brand he smoked. I never let on that I knew. I didn't want to embarrass him or upset him. While his spying made me feel a little uneasy, I never realized it was wrong. I thought it was his way of showing me how much he cared. He always questioned where I had been and who I had been with. He was overly obsessive and extremely jealous. He constantly accused me of being with other guys.

This one time Kyle and I were sitting at a stoplight and I casually looked over at the car beside us. I never noticed who was driving. I was just looking at the car. It was nice, sleek and racy looking. I was thinking how fun it would be to have one. From out of nowhere, Kyle grabbed my head and smashed it into the passenger window. Then he pressed my face up against the glass screaming obscenities and accusing me of staring at the guy in the car. "You want to look at him, bitch? Then take a good look! See him? Is that what you want?" He yelled as he pressed my face harder into the glass. It scared me so badly that it took years for me to be able to look anyone in the eyes. Whenever I would meet someone, I would instinctively put my head and eyes downcast, never making eye contact.

My best friend in high school was a boy named James. We were very close and I cared a great deal for him. But I only felt friendship. For James it became more. He wrote me a letter one day confessing that his feelings for me had changed. I don't know why I kept that letter. If I would have known the pain it would cause me later, I would have thrown it away. Kyle found the letter. I tried to explain that it was nothing, but he didn't believe me. This was the first time he beat me. Unfortunately, it wasn't the last. That night he turned into someone I never knew before. For the first time since we had met, I was afraid of him— yet, I was even more afraid of losing him.

Over the course of that entire day and into the night, this man beat me savagely and without restraint. Kyle grabbed his knife and scored it down my forearm. Although he didn't cut deep enough for stitches, he did push hard enough that it burned and bled, as he screamed in my ear, "You love me? Do you love me, Alyssa?"

Later that night, we were in his car and he hit me repeatedly while trying to stay on the road. When we came to a deserted part of town in the middle of nowhere, he leaned over suddenly and opened my door, pushing me out of the car while it was still moving. I rolled on the gravel and pavement for what seemed like forever. When I realized he was gone, I was relieved, yet terrified because I had no idea where I was.

My body was battered and broken and I was covered in blood. My heart was crushed; my spirit defeated. I sobbed as I walked around in the dark trying to find my way. Then I heard the all-too familiar sounds of a car as it slowly approached. I tried desperately to hide, but there was no place for me to go. The headlights found me and I wondered if death was near.

Kyle pulled the car over and parked. Then he started walking towards me. I heard strange noises coming from his direction—the closer he got, the louder the noises. It was then that I realized the sounds were actually pitiful sounds of sobbing—and they were coming from him! Kyle let it all go. He cried without reservation or embarrassment. He told me that he loved me.

"Please forgive me, Alyssa. I'm so sorry. I just love you so much. I promise I will never hurt you again," he pleaded. I didn't know what else to do, so I forgave him. He was all I had—and he loved me when no one else did.

Not long afterward, I moved in with him. I could barely afford to take care of myself while going to school, and my mom made it clear I wasn't welcome in her home. It seemed I had little choice in the matter, so I accepted his offer. He had temporarily stopped hurting me physically, for which I was very grateful, but his obsession for me continued. Kyle's mother would see the way he treated me, but she assured me that he loved me very much. She also told me to never tell anyone, especially the police.

One day, while Kyle and I were in the grocery store shopping with his mom, we got into an argument and he called me a slut. Then he announced at the top of his voice, "Your shorts are too short!" I wanted to crawl into one of the empty bins and cover myself in produce. His mom did her best to ignore him, but his name-calling grew worse and more offensive. Suddenly, without warning, Kyle walked up to me, grabbed my shorts, and literally ripped them off me. His mom's quick reaction saved me from even more embarrassment as she held the shorts up on me, covered me with her body, and led me back to the car. When we got home, she attempted to sew them back together as best as she could. "It will be okay, Alyssa. You have to try to let it go. He just loves you so much," she whimpered. The words she meant for comfort did nothing for me. I was mortified and terribly hurt.

Kyle continued to follow me wherever I went, lurking in the

shadows from afar. At night, when he would come home, he would always demand a full account of my day; where I had been, who I had been with, and what I had done. I never understood his demands because he already knew what I did and where I went, but still I obeyed. He also tapped the phone lines so he could monitor my conversations; who I talked to and when. I was a prisoner in his own personal prison, under his control with no other prisoners around. He alienated me from my family and I was not allowed to have any friends.

From the time I was 13, Kyle had me convinced when he told me, "You are nothing, Alyssa! No one will ever want you! No one could love you the way I do." Funny thing was I believed him. I believed I was nothing without him. I believed I had nothing to offer anyone and that no one could possibly love me. My self-esteem was shot. There was nothing left. I started having suicidal thoughts again. I was certain that death had to be better than this.

It wasn't long before his hurtful comments began to border on threats to my life. "Don't ever leave me," he would scream. "I would die, and so will you. I will not let you live without me." In my confused, deranged state of mind, this much I knew; I loved Kyle as much as I feared him. It made no sense, but it was truth.

When the beatings started up again, it became a cycle I could almost predict; he would become enraged and hit me, say he was sorry, tell me he loved me and promise to never do it again. Then he would beg for my forgiveness—and of course, I would always forgive him. What else could I do? Then it would start all over again. I don't know why I lived this way, but I clung to him like a life raft—as if my life truly depended on it. I believed that if I were to ever let go, I would drown.

I hid the secrets and shame of the life we shared from my family and friends. It was far too painful, and I was too embarrassed for them to know how weak I was. And this was exactly how Kyle wanted it. It was his plan all along. I was pathetic. I did not have the self esteem or the willpower to escape his abuse—so I stayed.

When I look back I realize how much I tried to make light of the things Kyle said and did to me. It was the only way I could emotionally deal with my situation. In school I was greatly troubled and went into a downward spiral very quickly. My mom finally intervened.

She decided I needed to get far away from everything and everyone. So she sent me to the Philippines—a country where I didn't know anyone and had nothing to lose. I was only 15. I couldn't even communicate with the locals because I didn't know their language. I never felt more alone in my life. I thought it was my mother's way of getting rid of me—as if sweeping my entire existence under the carpet—out of sight and out of mind from everyone.

My mother had arranged for me to stay with some of her distant relatives; some I had never even met and others I hadn't been around much at all, including her mother. I felt lost and rejected as I tried desperately to live in a world that was completely foreign, with people I knew nothing about. The short time I was there, I made a few "friends." However, these were not ones I would ever write home about. They never cared for me or for my wellbeing.

Every one of them was an addict, and I eventually I became one, too.

Hooked on crystal meth, I lost 35 pounds in six months. I spent my 16th birthday smoking dirty crystal off of foil sheets, high and oblivious to people who wanted to take advantage of me. Reckless and abandoned, I didn't care about anything or anyone, especially myself. I was supposed to go to school, but never made it. I was falling fast without a net. My grandmother could see that things weren't right and would plead with my mom to fly me back home. Finally after six long months, my mom relented.

When I came back home to the United States, I was a wreck and went through major withdrawals. I felt as if I were right back where I started—alone. No one cared. No one wanted me. There was only one person in my entire life who had ever claimed to truly love me, or at least this was what I believed at the time. I was desperate. I couldn't take another heartache or disappointment. It was at this time that I made one of the worst decisions I could possibly make. I called Kyle and he came running—back into my arms as if nothing had ever changed. In no time at all, he had slipped into the routine of physically and emotionally abusing me, and it broke my heart.

I went to visit my sister Nicole one day. My cousin Penny was there and she began talking to me about the Lord. I went through the motions of telling her that there was no way God could love someone like me. I remember asking her, "If God is so good, then why do bad things always happen?" Penny answered, "God is good, Alyssa. But the world is not. He loves us enough to let us make our own choices, but unfortunately those choices often lead to unfavorable consequences. Like what's happened to you." There was no doubt I had made some pretty horrific choices, so I proceeded to ask her more questions. And with each answer Penny gave, I was drawn to them like bees to honey, as if they could very well be my lifeline for hope and a future.

In 1998, I accepted Jesus Christ as my Savior, which means I asked Him into my heart and to be Lord of my life. I knew I would spend eternity with Him in heaven, and this gave me more hope and comfort than I'd ever known before. Kyle and I were still together. I remember constantly praying for him; for the Lord to soften his heart so that he could feel what I was feeling. But it was not to be. Kyle constantly mocked me in my faith. He was cruel in putting me down for my new beliefs. I realize now that he probably felt threatened, because I finally knew that there was Someone who truly did love me—for me. Someone who wanted me! Who accepted me! It didn't matter what I had done in the past. Jesus loved me more than anyone ever could, and He forgave me.

It wasn't long after that I finally found the courage to leave Kyle. However, the courage was short-lived when I found out I was pregnant. Kyle wanted me to stay with him. I began to pray for him—and for us. Several months later, after giving birth to our daughter Zoey, we were married. I wanted to try to make a life with Kyle for our daughter's sake. He continued to belittle me, and I continued to pray for him. I was miserable. Kyle made me feel incompetent, not only in keeping our home, but also being his wife. He made me feel fat and unattractive.

At this point in my life, I was still very new as a Christian. I didn't know what I was supposed to be doing as a child of God. Often times I was so torn between trying to meet Kyle's expectations as his wife, and my new faith in pleasing my Lord. Depression hit me hard and it started to spiral out of control. A lot of it had to do with me not being able to lose the weight I had gained carrying my daughter. I weighed 180 pounds and was desperate to drop the unwanted weight, not only to please Kyle, but to gain confidence in myself.

Through bouts of bulimia and long periods of starving myself I was able to get back down to my pre-pregnancy weight of 110 pounds, and I did it in four months. But it still wasn't enough for Kyle. He still put me down and made me feel worthless, like only he could do. I knew he would never change and I would never be able to please him. It was at this time I decided once again to leave him. But before I could actually walk away, I found out I was pregnant with our second child. Oh dear God, now what? I thought.

I was beyond devastated. I didn't know what to do. I was trapped in an unhealthy marriage and once again forced to stay. I didn't understand how it happened. I was taking my birth control pills every day. They were supposed to work. But all too soon I found out why they didn't. Kyle had made laughing comments about him taking my birth control pills out of their container, leading me to believe I had taken them already. No wonder I was pregnant again. I am so ashamed to say this, but I had even thought about having an abortion. In the end, taking my child's life was something I just could not do. I loved the precious life growing inside of me with all my heart, but I often asked myself, "What kind of world will this baby be born into?" I went through my pregnancy to full term, but it was in complete and utter sadness.

A few months before our second daughter was born, I overheard Kyle talking to one of his friends on the phone. He was putting me down as usual, telling his friend how disgusted he was by me and admitting that he didn't want to have sex with me anymore. His words cut me deep. When I confronted him about it, he immediately began packing his things. Maybe it is better that he leaves, I thought to myself. It would definitely be less stressful. Just as this thought came to mind, Kyle reached down and picked up Zoey who was only a year old. I realized then that he had planned to take her too. I completely lost it. "No! Please, Kyle, don't take my baby! Don't take Zoey!" I screamed and tried grabbing her from his arms. But he wouldn't let her go.

At this point it became a tug of war, both of us literally pulling our beloved daughter away from one another. Zoey started crying hysterically and fell to the floor. Kyle slapped me hard and then slammed me up against a wall. I looked down at Zoey who was watching her father beat on me as she frantically cried out for her momma. Kyle finally let go of me and left. I was shaken, but my poor, sweet Zoey was inconsolable. I held her in my arms, soothing her with my words as we both sat on the floor and cried together.

Not too long after Kyle had left, I began to cramp and was terrified for my unborn child. When the pain increased, I called my mom and asked for her help. Her response to me was cold and calloused. "I just got off the phone with Kyle. He told me everything. You need to work out your problems with him on your own. Leave me out of this." Then she hung up. I also reached out to my oldest sister who had always been there for me, but she had also received a call from Kyle. Nicole told me point blank that she couldn't help me either. I was dumb founded and panic stricken. I didn't know what to do.

A short time later, as I cradled a sleeping Zoey, Kyle came back home and took me to the hospital. The doctor informed us that I was going into pre-term labor. They were able to stop the contractions, but they kept me overnight as a precaution. That night as I lay in my hospital bed, I knew that leaving Kyle was inevitable. A few months after the birth of our second daughter Kayla, I made the choice to walk away.

After almost ten years of his emotional and physical abuse, one thing kept coming to mind that made me realize I could not be with this man any longer. There was no way I could ever have my daughters growing up and watching the way Kyle mistreated me. I wanted my daughters to expect more from their future husbands; to know that they were cherished, and loved, and protected by them. How could they ever learn this lesson in our home when their own father mistreated me as his wife and as the mother to his children?

My family was outraged when they learned that I had called things off with Kyle. I became an outcast and was avoided by everyone—mostly by my mom. She argued that Kyle was a good provider and that I was lucky to have him. When I finally told her the truth about the abuse, she didn't believe me. Then she said, "But even if it's true, Alyssa, he said he was sorry and that he wouldn't hit you anymore." This was when I realized Kyle had admitted to her that he had hit me, but I was still the bad guy for leaving. "You need to get back together with him," my mom screamed. When I rejected her advice, she told me that I was dead to her and she refused to have anything to do with me.

It took almost two years for my mother to come around again. During that time, I worked two jobs just to make it financially in order to raise my two daughters. There were many days that I didn't have enough money to feed myself, because I was living paycheck to paycheck just to buy formula and diapers. From lack of food, I lost even more weight and was put on anti-depressants. I had creditors calling me at all hours of the day and night, at home and at work, demanding payment. I couldn't handle the pressure any longer. I finally broke down and filed for bankruptcy.

During that first year of separation, I was always looking over my shoulder. I just knew Kyle would find some way to hurt me or have me killed because he still followed me everywhere. He was trying to either intimidate me or to just obsessively stalk me. Whatever it was, it worked. I was terrified!

By this time I was so angry with God. I was always asking Him, "Why? Why, God? Why is this happening? If You love me so much, why are You doing this?" The empty void and sadness in my heart ran deep. I attempted to fill this void by being extremely promiscuous with several men, allowing anyone to take advantage of me in my lonely brokenness. At one point I had sex with two different men in less than 24 hours. Then it was the drugs. Whenever the opportunity arose, I started doing them again—any and all—whatever was available. I also began drinking heavily. I was miserable and I knew I needed help. And help came in the form of a Savior.

One night I just laid it all out there. I confessed to the Lord the sinful life I was leading. I cried out to Him in desperation and prayed for Him to comfort me and to give me strength. I told Him I was willing to stop trying to take control and give my life to Him—completely. I told Him I would accept His will for me, whatever it was. I prayed He would bless me with a godly man, or to comfort me if His will was for me to be alone. Because of His ultimate grace, my Abba Father broke the chains that bound me to my sin and made me alive again. A month later, I met Matt—my soon-to-be husband and life partner forever.

While I knew Matt was my special gift of love and companionship from God, we both realized that God had started to reveal in me that I had some serious healing to do before we could ever get married. During this time I still suffered from a posttraumatic stress disorder caused by my ex-husband, as well as the night terrors, when I would scream and lash out violently. Feeling unsure and unsteady, Matt and I postponed our original wedding date by six months to attend pre-marital counseling with our pastor. It was at that time that the Lord led me to a ministry called *Healing Hearts*. Within this ministry I was able to find the healing I needed—and the forgiveness I longed for. Kyle had caused me so much pain—both physically and emotionally, but the deepest pain was the abandonment I felt from my mom.

I love my mom and I have forgiven her, even though we have our fair share of disagreements now and then. However, this could only happen through God's grace. I realized that the power I believed she had to hurt me wasn't there anymore. My mom has her side of the story as well as the path she has chosen for herself.

As of this day, she has chosen to walk outside the path of God's grace, and without God's direction and guidance. We see each other often, and I feel called to love on her and shower her with unconditional grace, for that is what the Bible tells us to do in Matthew 15:4 "Honor your father and mother..." And so I will.

I never thought our relationship would be where it is today, especially with all those horribly painful years I suffered because of her ignorance. But God cut through that sorrow and hurt that had been so deeply seeded in my soul—He came to my rescue and healed me. I pray constantly that my mom will someday experience the peace which I have found in having a personal relationship with my Creator—a peace that surpasses all understanding.

For so many years I held onto the unanswered question of, "If You loved me so much, God, why did You let so many horrible things happen to me?" Now I know that God didn't let anything happen to me. It was the sinful nature of this world that took hold of me, and God was there with me through it all. In reality, the pain of my past actually turned out to be a blessing. Each time I suffered or was in despair, it was like leaving a trail of breadcrumbs that could lead me back to my Abba Father. Then, in His time and in His way, He rescued me.

In John 11:35 it says, "Jesus wept." All those years, He wept for me. I know now that the events in my life are a testament to God's love and redemption, and that my witness can be used to serve Him and bring others who are going through what I have gone through to the Lord. I pray that one day soon I will lead a *Healing Hearts* ministry of my own. In Isaiah 61, it says that God Himself will restore the crumbling foundations of your life. He will give you beauty for ashes. He will provide redemption. He has for me. He can for you. Don't give up. Victory is yours if you seek Him and then trust Him with all your heart.

Yes, Matt and I did get married and God blessed us with two more daughters, Selah and Rachel. Matt loves Zoey and Kayla as his own and they are crazy about him. After all these years, I finally have the family I've always wanted and I feel loved like never before. I am blessed. Life is good. And my God is faithful. To Him be the glory forever.

Forgiven

As I sit here writing from this dingy concrete room I now call home, I have a lot of time to reflect on all the mistakes I've made and the lasting regrets that can never be undone. My life now, compared to what it used to be, is like comparing Heaven and Hell—and this is Hell.

When I was 15, I made the most detrimental decision of my life, one that I will pay for as long as I am alive—both emotionally as well as geographically. I am in prison, 14 years down, 36 years to go. I got 50 to life. There isn't a day that goes by that I don't think about "that day" and the pain I caused so many innocent people from the moment I chose to follow through with "the plan." If it were at all possible for me to take any of it back, I would in a heartbeat. I am so sorry for the pain I caused everyone involved. Even though I've made peace with God and I know He has forgiven me; inside, my guilt is never ending and will be until I take my last breath here on earth. Let me take you back a few years—30 to be exact.

I was born in Frederick, Maryland in 1986, but soon moved to Fort Detrick, home to the U.S. Army Medical Research & Material Command. My mother had joined the U.S. Army and in June 1989, her unit was deployed to the Middle East. When she came home on leave that Christmas, she and my father decided it would be best for them to get a divorce. She went back to complete her assignment and my dad took care of me and my older brother, Michael. The next year, when her tour of duty was over and she came home for good, the divorce became final. I stayed with my dad and Michael went to live with my mom.

When I was six, my dad and I settled in together in the small close-knit community of Brunswick and life was good. Some of my fondest memories as a child were made there. I had a lot of good friends, did quite well in school, and felt blessed that I could share it all with my best friend—my dad—who was always there for me, no matter what. I played all types of sports; football, basketball, baseball, and soccer. But if I could choose one as my favorite, it would be baseball. I played for many years and my dad was my coach. We had a very special bond, one that is still strong—even today.

Because we attended church regularly, I knew from an early age that God was real. My dad always prayed in front of me and with me, making me aware that there was, indeed, a Higher

Power. But he was never one to shove it down my throat. I didn't always pay attention to what he was saying, but somewhere deep inside me, his words penetrated through and seeds were being planted.

I was in middle school running for class president when my dad announced that we were moving to 29 Palms, California. My grandparents were there and my dad wanted to be closer to them. I can't even begin to describe my disappointment. I was crushed, but we moved anyway. I enjoyed being with my grandparents and ended up making some great friends as well. Our family found a Baptist church close by and we started going every weekend. I also became very involved in their youth group where some of my friends also attended. We were happy. It wasn't Brunswick, but it wasn't bad.

When I was cast to play the role of Linus in one of the school plays, I met this kid named Brian and we became inseparable. Brian suffered from a crippling muscle disease, but it didn't make any difference in our friendship. I was with him almost every day and soon I hardly noticed his handicap. But this wasn't the case for some of the other kids who felt it their duty to harass, bully and tease Brian because he was different from them. And because he was my friend, I felt the need to protect him. Brian was grateful to have me around and I was glad to be able to help whenever I could. Our friendship grew and we became the best of friends. But a year later tragedy struck and I was devastated. Brian was killed in a bus accident. I never had anyone close to me die before and the pain was almost unbearable.

Then, during the summer of 2000, we moved again to Santee, California near San Diego, and I didn't like it at all. Although it was not my desire to move again, my dislike for Santee wasn't because I didn't want to go. It was because of some of the people who lived there. They seemed cold and uncaring, and the kids were downright cruel.

That September, I started my freshman year at Santana High School and thus began a nightmare to which I never awoke. Although I tried very hard to fit in, I never felt wanted or accepted from the beginning. At the time, I was a scrawny 5'5" and barely weighed 110 pounds soaking wet, making me an easy target for some of the students' entertainment. I was tormented, teased, and harassed constantly—mostly by upper classmen. Sometimes it was just mean and hurtful slandering, but after a while, it turned physical and, every so often, even violent.

I was slugged in the face repeatedly and personal things were taken from me—my backpack, skateboard, money, etc. I was also pushed into the swimming pool fully clothed. Then when I tried to get to the edge to climb out, I was smacked with a wet towel and shoved back in. I even had lit cigarette butts thrown at me, and several times I was actually set on fire at the cuffs of my pants or the hood of my sweatshirt.

Most of the abuse and bullying was done on the school campus, but not once did anyone do anything to stop it. I later learned that many of these incidents were recorded on video, but no one from administration ever came forward. I think it was probably because they would have had to take some of the responsibility for what eventually happened and that was something they were just not willing to do.

I was bullied, off and on, throughout my freshman year, from the first day of school in September 2000, until the first week of March the following year. I never told my teachers or anyone in administration—not even my dad. To be honest, I was too embarrassed about it and didn't want to be seen as weak and wimpy by running to an adult every time I needed to be rescued. My tormentors also threatened to do worse things to me if I did tell anyone. What could possibly be worse than being set on fire? I wasn't sure, nor was it something I wanted to find out. So instead, I chose silence. For six months, I did nothing but cower and let them have their way with me. Then one day, I got angry.

Unfortunately, the choices I made during that regretful time in my life, found me with some very unsuitable company. Being with these guys was where I learned how to mask my pain. I started doing drugs—everyday—any drug I could get my hands on; uppers, downers, pot, coke, and ecstasy, most of which I could find at school. Although I had experimented with a few drugs before this, it was never done on a regular basis until I started being bullied.

I had a couple of close buddies that I hung out with quite a bit. AJ, Josh and I were the "misfits" of Santana High and, when we were "high", it didn't bother us in the least. I confided in them about what was going on and, although they weren't being bullied themselves, they told me they wanted to help me get even. The last straw came the Saturday night before that fateful day, when the three of us were cruising around downtown and were pulled over by the cops.

My buddy, Josh, was busted for having drugs in his possession. His step-dad, who had been molesting both Josh and me on a regular basis, said he wouldn't tell his mother if Josh, in turn, would perform a sexual favor on him. Even though his request wasn't surprising, it was what finally pushed me over the edge. If you can't trust the adults in your life and you're constantly being harassed by your peers, what chance was there for me to have any type of a normal life?

It was at this point that I just wanted to die for a better lack of alternatives—but AJ and Josh came up with different plan. It definitely was not a good idea that we were high the night "the plan" was devised. In fact, I was still high that next Monday morning when I got to school. The three of us were supposed to meet in the parking lot, but my buddies never showed. By that time it really didn't matter. I was armed and ready—and was completely out of my mind! You just don't know what the mind is capable of making you do when it's clouded by drugs and anger—a very deadly combination.

Before I left the house, I grabbed my dad's gun from the gun cabinet. The only reason why he even had a gun was because we had recently been robbed. He showed me where he hid the key just in case there was ever a need to protect myself, which was exactly what I planned to do. I took out his .22-caliber revolver, closed the cabinet door, and then walked the short distance to my school.

When I walked through the doors of Santana High that morning, I had the revolver in my backpack. At first I just wanted to get some attention. I was so tired of being bullied and teased. I desperately wanted to have a normal life at school and to be accepted and liked, but a handful of kids had already wrecked that for me.

I went into the boys' bathroom and had briefly considered shooting myself, but there was a freshman kid in there that I knew, so instead, he became my target. After contemplating the situation for about five minutes, I took the gun out of my backpack, pointed it at him, and fired. He fell to the floor and I walked out. It was too late to change the plan now. The damage had already begun. The bell rang and the halls filled with students walking around in their own little worlds, laughing and enjoying themselves. Once again the anger stirred inside of me. That was when I held up the gun and pulled the trigger.

I wasn't aiming at anyone in particular—I just found myself shooting and shooting and shooting. Twenty-four shots later, I stopped. It was over. I went back into the bathroom where I thought about killing myself again, but by that time the police had already arrived. I knew it was only a matter of time before they would come get me, so I just stood there and waited. One of the officers approached me and asked if there were any other shooters. "It's just me," I assured him. "Just me."

Then they cuffed me and took me away. I didn't get a chance to tell my dad what had happened. The police called him at work and he came to the Santee Sheriff Station where I was being questioned by the FBI. My dad wasn't allowed in the room during their interrogation. Once they were through, they let me see him.

When he walked in, I fell into his arms and cried like a baby. "I'm sorry, dad. I'm just so sorry! I didn't mean to do it!" I blubbered. He held me and comforted me just like I knew he would. "Everything will be okay," he said. But I knew he didn't believe it—not for a minute. He was devastated and I knew I hurt him more than he would ever admit.

The pain and suffering I caused my father that day was and still is my greatest regret. It absolutely crushed him, along with all the dreams he had for me. He was the best parent anyone could ever have and he didn't deserve any of this.

By days' end, the counts were in: Two dead, 13 injured, including a teacher and a school security guard. It still doesn't seem real to me—even today. I was interrogated for hours. They just kept asking me "Why?" But I never went into any details of what was really going on at Santana High. I never once mentioned the intensity of the bullying and abuse I had to face several times a week. I just briefly touched upon my unhappiness and being picked on, but I didn't want anyone else to be hurt because of me—so I never told. And like I said before, it made me feel weak and helpless, as if I had no backbone and couldn't take care of myself—even though the torture, at times, was often unbearable.

It wasn't until later that I was informed about all the damage I had done. It was all over the local and national news, especially after what had happened at Columbine two years before. No, I didn't do it because of what happened there. I was just fed-up and so depressed, and I wanted it all to just go away! It was almost as if I didn't have a choice.

I still don't remember that day very well, nor do I remember all the questions I was asked by the cops and the FBI. But the realization of it all hit me like a hurricane a short time later, as I sat all alone in my cell. I broke down and cried for every last one of those that I had hurt; the victims, their families and loved ones, and my family, too. That was March 5, 2001. I had just turned 15. After I was interrogated, they took me to juvenile hall until I was sentenced the next year.

I went back to court on June 20, 2002, where I pled guilty to all charges and without a fight. I didn't have a trial because I didn't think I deserved one. I never mentioned the bullying or the videos to the judge, nor did any of the other people who knew about them. I never saw the videos myself and I assume they are still in the sheriff's custody.

On August 15, 2002, I was sentenced to 50 years to life in prison. The judge ordered me to serve my time in the Youth Offender Program at Tehachapi State Prison north of Los Angeles until my 18th birthday.

Once I arrived at Tehachapi, I never caused any problems. I guess you could say I was a model inmate. I did anything I could to pass the time. I eventually graduated from high school, enrolled in some college courses, became adept in the Japanese art of origami, and marked my growth on the wall of my cell. When I was taken into custody, I was 5′5″ tall and weighed 110 pounds. While incarcerated at Tehachapi, I grew to nearly 6 feet and topped the scales at 150 pounds.

My real mother only came to see me a couple times. My dad and step-mom came at least once a month at first. Then, because of the miles in between, they came whenever they could, as did my grandparents. The rest of the time was spent reading and writing letters to have California Proposition 21, which allowed children under 21 to be tried as adults, declared unconstitutional. But to date, this fight has been unsuccessful.

On August 17, 2002, I was interviewed by Diane Sawyer for her show "Prime Time" on ABC. I was later informed that they had received more letters and emails about that interview than they had ever received about any show they had aired. Either way, it still didn't help in my fight with Prop 21.

Whenever my grandparents would come to see me, they would pray over me as they had always done when I was younger. One day after they left, I felt lonelier than ever, so got down on my knees and said a prayer. Later that night, as I lay in my cell, I felt this tugging at my heart and a Voice began to converse with me. The feeling inside was incredible and I knew it was God! Much to my surprise, He assured me I would never be alone no matter where I was and that He loved me and had forgiven me, even with what I had done. This was very hard for me to comprehend or to accept at first. How could anyone love me or forgive me when I couldn't love or forgive myself?

It took me a while to understand the concept of Jesus and His unconditional love. What I learned was that over two thousand years ago, God sent His Son, Jesus, to the earth to die on the cross for all our sins. Then three days later, He was resurrected to give us eternal life if we accept, repent, and believe (John 3:16). How could this be? I thought. I murdered two people and hurt a dozen others. I am the worst of sinners! But, strange as it may sound, I wasn't to God. He knew my heart and He knew how remorseful I felt. Even someone who has murdered can go to Heaven! If we repent and confess our sins, and then ask God to forgive us of them all, we will spend eternity in His presence.

When I thought about how long eternity was and how long my life on earth actually would be, it was a no-brainer. Earth life... about 80 years; eternity...more years than anyone could possibly count, more than all the stars in the heavens. I wanted to know more about this incredible God who was willing to take me as I was and love me anyway. So, along with the college courses offered at the prison, I enrolled in a Bible class.

As I read through His Book, I learned that some of God's own people had committed murder and still He used them in extraordinary ways and for His glory—Moses killed an Egyptian after watching the guy beat up a Hebrew friend of his, and it was Moses who God used to part the Red Sea (leading the Israelites to safety), and to write the Ten Commandments. Saul murdered thousands of Christians and then later became the Apostle Paul, authoring many of the books in the Bible. Not that I am anything like Moses or Paul, but I knew God even could use someone like me to better His cause if I were willing to give Him my whole life.

I wasn't going anywhere anytime soon and had more time on my hands than most. So, as I read His words, I began sharing what I had read and learned with anyone who would listen. I'm not sure if I will ever understand fully why God loves us so much, but I don't think we have to understand it, as long as we believe and put our trust in His will for us. Our finite brains aren't capable of putting it all together, but to know and feel that we have a God who watches over us and who loves us—no matter how undeserving we are—is all He expects.

I know what you're thinking, that most of us in prison have nothing better to do than to read the Bible and get all holy and preachy. And I'm sure there are those who do just that, claiming they know Jesus but then don't do anything different with their lives. But they are only fooling themselves—not God. He knows our hearts and if change doesn't happen there, it doesn't happen at all!

A month after my 18th birthday, I was transferred to Calipatria State Prison for adults, where I was once again a model inmate for the next four years. I never caused any trouble and always did what I was told. I made a lot of friends and was about as happy as I could be under the circumstances, especially when I reconnected with Megan, a girl that I knew in high school.

Over time, my friendship with Megan blossomed into a deep love and respect for one another, and we eventually became engaged. When we first began "catching feelings" for one another, I tried to push her away because this (being in prison) sucks. I told her, "This is the best it will ever get Megan—some visits and phone calls. That's it!" But she said it didn't matter. "I don't care, Andy. I want to be with you. I love you."

We were supposed to be married in 2008, in front of my parents and grandparents, and all of those inside the prison who had befriended the both of us. But then, out of the blue, I was transferred to another prison near Fresno, California—about four hours farther for Megan to visit. I did not want to go, but I had no choice.

During those first few months at the Pleasant Valley State Prison in Coalinga, California, I was overwhelmed with grief and depression. I didn't know what to do or how I was going to make it through the next 40 years of my life. It takes stamina, focus, and a great deal of willpower to get through each day in prison, and I tried everything to stay busy. I got into sports again— playing football and baseball whenever we were allowed outside. I also worked out every chance I could. At 6'5", I was pretty sure I was finally done growing.

I took jobs in the kitchen, library, etc. I also did some janitorial work and whatever else I could do to get me through the days. But the nights were the hardest when I had more time to think about Megan. Because of the distance that now separated us, she could only come every few months instead of once a month, but at least it gave me something to look forward to. However, when it was time for her to leave, I was heartbroken.

It would take weeks for me to get used to the mundane world I lived in before she came, which in turn, sent me back into a deep depression. This went on for more than a year, and then to my surprise, another prison suddenly became available. But this time the transfer was offered to anyone who wanted to go—so I jumped on it.

I spent the next few years at the Ironwood State Prison in Blythe, California near San Diego, which was so convenient for Megan and my family to visit. They came often and I felt very blessed, and life was good again. Soon I was moved to Chuckawalla Valley State Prison right down the street from Ironwood, and I settled into a very comfortable routine for a couple more years.

Then one day I was informed that I was being transferred to SATF (Substance Abuse Treatment Facility) in Corcoran, CA. I hated that place so much that I waited until ANYTHING became available, which I knew had to be better than where I was. To my surprise, the next available transfer was the very same prison where I had been placed 14 years ago—right after I was convicted.

Today I'm serving time at the California Correctional Institution (CCI) in Tehachapi, California near Bakersfield. I do not like this place and, even though I'm not in the same yard as I was before, it still sucks. All I want to do is get back to Chuckawalla so I can see Megan and my family more often. But the Lord wants me here for a reason, so I will be patient and see what direction He takes me.

My dad and Megan visit as often as possible, though it's not nearly as convenient. I haven't seen my grandparents in four years. It's just too hard for them to travel so far, which is another reason why I want to be closer.

After many years of transfers and delays, Megan and I were finally able to "tie the knot" during a ceremony here at the prison. My dad, stepmom, aunt, brother, sister-in-law, mom, and two of my buddies came to witness our vows and to celebrate with us.

Megan and I were first to go up as there were five other couples in line getting married that same day. We said our "I do's" and took lots of pictures. Afterward, all of us hung out together for a couple hours laughing and reminiscing and, for a brief moment, it felt as if time had stood still.

Then visiting hours were over and everyone said their goodbyes; my wife, my family, and my friends left the prison and drove home, and I went back to my cell where time passed at an agonizingly slow pace. Megan's love and support means more to me than I can say and I know she will continue to be there for me in all that I do and all that I am within these prison walls.

My desire is to someday be a social worker and help kids get through the hard times—that is, if I ever get out of here. I finally earned my A.A. in Science and in Mathematics. I've also taken several more Bible study classes over the years so that I can be more confident to share the Gospel to other inmates without stumbling over my words—or His. I am hopeful that I can plant some seeds for Christ all around the prison.

These days I spend my time playing music and studying God's word. We have church services once a week in the yard and I play guitar on the worship team, which makes being here a little more tolerable. For my 25th birthday, my stepmom bought me my first guitar and I've only been playing for about five years. Fortunately, I've had some really great teachers and they taught me well. When people ask me if I sing too, I tell them, "Yes, I sing solo—'so low' that you can't hear me."

The hell I live in today is very real, but I know it's only

temporary, even if I have to do the entire 50-years-to-life sentence. The Hell in the Bible is also very real, but it's forever to those who choose to ignore God's free offer of salvation. We've all heard about the horrors of Hell; excruciating pain, lasting regret, and a darkness never known before—which lasts for all eternity! My question is, why would anyone chose Hell as their destiny when Heaven is just as real?

I can tell you with all certainty that what I've learned about God's grace is true. I couldn't live this life here in prison without knowing that there is a better life waiting for me someday. And even if I weren't incarcerated, life outside these walls isn't always that great either, as I am sure many of you can agree. There will always be tears, pain, suffering and death. But with Jesus in your heart—no matter who you are, where you are, or what you've done—He will forgive you if you turn to Him and ask. And all God's angels will rejoice, knowing that someday you will be with your Savior in Heaven.

Many people think that Heaven is only for those who are good. But they are wrong. Heaven is not for the good—it is for the forgiven. And I know without a doubt that I have been forgiven of the horrendous choices I made well over a decade ago. Had I known God when I was going through all that pain at Santana High, I would have never felt so alone nor so desperate to have harmed another soul. And even though I know that this incident was not part of God's original plan for me, He knew I was going to do it way before I did. But He also knew He would use it to bring Him glory one day, and that is what I am doing now—by telling all of you my story.

I hope that someone out there will read this and learn from the poor choices I've made, and not let what happened to me, happen to you. If someone is tormenting you, tell the authorities! Don't ignore it or try to fix it yourself. You cannot win! And if you're the one who's tormenting someone, back off! You don't have a clue what you're doing to them and the ramifications it could cause. Whatever happens will be just as much your fault as it is the fault of the person who takes matters into their own hands.

The life I'm living now is not what I had planned, but it is what it is. And the only way I can get through it is by holding onto the hope of knowing that "I can do all things through Christ who strengthens me", as the Apostle Paul wrote in Philippians 4:13 when he was in prison.

Some days are definitely better than others, but overall, because of my faith and Megan, and my father, family, and friends, I am doing pretty well—all things considered. There is great hope behind these walls knowing that someday, even with all that I've done wrong in my life I will be with my Savior in the next, for all eternity, which makes my life here on earth more bearable.

My fight against Prop 21 is still in the works. My attorney is trying to get it into juvenile court where he plans to bring all the bullying and videos to light. If this passes, I could be released sooner than the 50-year sentence I received—maybe even in the next few years. Don't get me wrong. I know what I did and it cannot go without punishment. The crime was horrible and I do not condone it nor do I want it to be taken lightly. However, under the circumstances of what I was dealing with at the time and only being 15 years old, I don't feel that I deserved the sentence I was given either. I think there is an answer somewhere in between. I just want the chance to finally tell my side of the story and then whatever happens after that, I will accept as God's will.

And if Prop 21 never comes to pass and I don't get another chance to be on the outside, I will cross that bridge when I come to it. I take one day at a time and lean on a very strong Savior because I know that I can do all things through Christ who strengthens me—and He does—everyday. I cannot thank Him enough.

But For His Grace, Go I

I was raised in Memphis, Tennessee by my devout Christian mother. There were four of us boys. I was the youngest. When I was born, my brothers were four, six and eight years old. Almost from the time I could walk, we all shared a bedroom together; two sets of bunks beds, four boys, in one room.

My father was there in a physical sense, but emotionally he was disconnected—as if being held hostage in an emotional prison. He was good at providing for his family but that was the extent of his fathering. He was never there for us; he never held us, or helped us. My father would leave for work at 4:30 in the morning and he didn't return until 6pm. When he came home he wanted silence so that he could watch television and unwind. When he spoke, we listened. He never hurt us or abused us but, clearly, he did not understand what fathers were supposed to do. Never once did he play with us, or throw a ball, or get involved in anything we did. Never once do I remember hearing him say, "I love you". Thank God for my mom. If not for her, I would have been even more of a mess than I was.

It was because of mother's upbringing that I had even the slightest knowledge of God. She was a Southern Baptist who attended church several times a week, listening to what I referred to as "hellfire and brimstone" teachings. This method of teaching caused me to see God as a perpetually angry, wrathful, and vengeful God who condemned people to Hell for the sheer enjoyment He got from it. It was frightening to think of God this way, especially for a kid my age.

My mom took all of us boys to church every Sunday morning and Wednesday night, as well as every time there was a revival. If the church doors were open, we went. However, my brothers would usually figure out a way to sneak out the back doors where they could smoke or get high so they didn't have to listen to the message. They rarely made it through the announcements before escaping.

Over the years, I was sent on church trips numerous times, and would be around other people at different church events and functions, but there was never a real relationship or connection with any of them—sadly, not even with God.

Throughout most of my life I was extremely insecure. I lacked self-confidence. I felt alone. My older brothers were twelve, fourteen and sixteen at the time, and they never wanted me around because I always told on them. They were a rebellious bunch, always doing something to get in trouble; drinking, partying, and doing drugs. I was just the annoying little brother who didn't fit in, and always tattled.

When I was seven, I started hanging around with a boy that was four years older than me, but I think emotionally he was younger than that, which was probably why we got along so well. We began doing fun things together. Suddenly, I no longer felt alone. I was getting the attention and companionship I wanted—but soon that wasn't enough.

It started out just playful teasing and experimenting like most kids do. Then it became more intimate. He did things to me that felt good. He gave me the attention I craved, which I mistook for love. He was filling a need that wasn't being met by my father or my church.

By the time I was eight, I had had my first sexual encounter with this boy. It was never forced and I never fought the idea but, in reality, this boy did take advantage. It was not something I chose. However, I never felt molested either. I wanted it to happen. If truth be told, I thought I was the one seducing him because I desired for it to happen again and again. He was paying attention to me. I felt important. It must be love. In fact, I realized later that this was the only time I ever felt loved—when sex was involved. However, before meeting this boy, I never thought about sex, or about men for that matter. I was so young that it had never crossed my mind.

This boy and I would go and hide, and I think I knew deep

down that what we were doing was wrong, or else why would we have to hide? It was never painful and I was with my most trusted friend. Nonetheless, he was the one who introduced it, though there was never any pressure on his part, nor resistance on mine. I was more than a willing participant, and I wanted it to happen as much as, or maybe even more than, he did. In fact, I was consumed with it.

Whenever my friend would come over, I would try very hard to recreate the situation again, because someone was finally paying attention to me. I was a little boy obsessed with that experience happening again and again as I played it over and over in my mind—because to me, it was love. He and I were actually only "together" a couple times, but I never forgot that feeling of pleasing, euphoric bliss. I could think of nothing else. Sex meant love and I wanted more. This was the beginning of my tumultuous existence for the next 35 years.

At a church revival when I was 12 years old, I said a prayer during an altar call. This was what people did when they wanted to give their lives to Jesus. A man told me if I would pray then I wouldn't go to Hell. So I did. Who wants to go to Hell? Not me! However, I never really believed or understood about Jesus or what He did on the cross. I knew He had died, but I didn't understand why. I basically wanted to be a good person but there was no real faith. I never made any changes, and nothing changed in my life. Yet, I went through life telling others that I was saved, and believing it. However, my actions told an entirely different story.

I was smoking by the age of eight; drinking at ten; using cocaine at fourteen. By this time, my attraction to men had become an obsession. My oldest brother (who was gay) was taking me to gay bars when I was thirteen. I saw it all in there... perversion, deviant, deliberate, provocative sex; all types of drugs—everywhere. The first few times I was shocked. Over time, it felt normal and people were paying attention to me.

My father was still disconnected from us. My mother had suffered nervous breakdowns throughout her life from the time I was about four. I remember her missing my fourth birthday party because she was in the hospital. This was my first experience of feeling abandoned. Grandma would come to stay with us (as would my aunts) for months at a time, but still I felt alone. I remember this day well because it was the first time I met Cynthia, who lived across the street.

My family had just moved into our new house. My grandma and my aunts threw a birthday party for me and they invited Cynthia to come. Although she was four years older, I considered her one of my best friend for the next 15 years. Later, Cindy and her family ended up moving to another city close by but we didn't see each other as much. I never told her about my attraction to men. I was too ashamed.

A few years later, I was out partying and I left this gay bar with a man, and we ended up at his place. When I came out of his room the next morning, Cindy was laying on the couch watching me come down the hall toward her. She shouted out my name. I tried to sneak back into the bedroom but she had seen me, and it was too late. The grief, guilt and shame covered me like a heavy wool blanket. Cindy knew. The stranger I had come home with was her roommate.

Not too long after this incident, Cindy overdosed on cocaine. Her funeral was held on my 19th birthday. She walked into my life when I was four, and I buried her 15 years later—to the day. I was one of her pallbearers. It was truly one of the worst days of my life.

I had several girlfriends in high school and into my early 20s. My relationships with them were real and intimate. Nonetheless, there were always men in between the girlfriends. I was trying very hard not to be gay; however, my cravings for men seemed overwhelming. I didn't know why I was so drawn to them. I had been taught that it was wrong, and I felt heavy guilt and embarrassment over the feelings, which created great conflict inside of me. I used the drugs and alcohol to mask the pain and to tune out the church, my family, and God. Sadly, I did not have the strength to handle my shame, and because of this I was living two separate lives and it was tearing me apart. My lust for men and porn had temporality satisfied, but it never filled me. The void inside was constant.

On my 18th birthday, I decided that killing myself was better than being in agony and living the lie of homosexuality. I felt so burdened. I actually had the gun in my lap and was sitting in a chair not five feet from my dad, who was sprawled out on the couch watching television. I was supposed to be at a birthday party that my mom had thrown for me at another location, but I wasn't in a party mood. I was tormented and depressed. I thought I was in love with another young man and I so desperately did not want to feel this way. I feared facing the truth of it all, and telling anyone what I had become. If I told, it would never be the same for me again. I wanted help, but I had no idea where to start.

That's when I thought suicide would be an easier way and much quicker than this slow death I was living inside. I sat in the chair in the living room and sobbed. My dad never once looked over at me. I know he heard me crying. He had to. "What's wrong with you?" he grumbled, but I couldn't tell him. The words were stuck deep in my throat. My father didn't push it, and I remembered feeling relieved. It was my excuse to get up and leave the room.

I went into my bedroom and crawled beneath the covers on my bed. Then I put the gun in my mouth. I laid there for the longest time with my finger on the trigger. I tasted the metal. It felt cold against my cheek. Soon it would be over. But I was a coward. I just couldn't do it.

A few hours later, my mom came home and she found me in bed. The gun was still in my hand—hidden under the covers. She heard me crying. "What's wrong, Billy? What happened?" she asked with great concern. But I couldn't tell her why I was crying. She'd never understand. "Please, honey, tell me what's wrong." By this time, she was crying too. My mom held me and stayed with me for two days to make sure I didn't harm myself. I never told her what was wrong and she never asked again. I prayed nearly every day afterward that I would die.

Sex was what I lived for. If anyone had told me they loved me, and we weren't having sex, I would think, "No way!" How could this be love? Even when I started having sex as I got older, the relationship (with men or women), no matter how long it lasted, had to have sex or it couldn't be love.

In my constant state of denial, I did not consider myself a homosexual. After all, I was sleeping with women too. But I always remembered that feeling the first time at eight years old and I wanted that emotional attachment over and over again. It made me feel complete. So that was what I aimed for—with anyone and everyone.

Later, I did what would soon become habit for me; I ran—as far away as I could. When I was 19, I moved to Dallas, Texas to get away from my family and the shame of my secrets. I attended Alcoholics Anonymous to stop using cocaine and alcohol. I ended up on prescription anti-depressants and tranquilizers because nothing had changed inside of me; my heart was still empty. I began to live openly in the gay community and eventually made my way to Metropolitan Community Church (MCC – Cathedral of Hope). This was the largest gay church in the world.

At this church I met other people like me. They had their hands in the air praising God and believing He was with them. They were being taught that God made them gay and as long as they were in a loving, monogamous relationship, it was okay to be involved in homosexuality. For the first time since a very young age, I didn't feel extreme shame and guilt. I felt normal. I was accepted. I thought the message they were preaching must be true. But I never studied the scriptures for myself. I bought the lie

...hook, line and sinker.

During this time, I met a wonderful man named Tom. We attended the same church and he would also frequent the gym I belonged to. He was older, mature, and extremely good looking. Tom was a prominent doctor in the area and it didn't take long for me to be swept off my feet. I fell head-over-heels in love with him. This man was controlling, but I didn't care. It actually fit his demeanor and his profession. I was intrigued, and he was wonderful to me. There wasn't anything he wouldn't do for me, or buy me.

Tom showered not only his affection on me, but he lavished me with gifts of every kind. He had a luxurious home in the city and I eventually moved in with him. We began a love story that lasted several years. We had all the bells and whistles the world had to offer. At the time, I assumed that all of this was a blessing from God. We had cars, homes, and money and our plush social life exceeded anything I ever imagined, but I still felt empty inside.

In an effort to quit living in two different worlds, I told my family about my being gay. The news grieved my mother greatly and my family attempted to share with me verse after verse in the Bible what God commanded. In my defense I would preach back to them what I had come to believe at MCC. I truly thought I was okay in the eyes of God, and there was nothing they could say or read to me that would change my mind.

To say I was finally happy would be a lie. Tom was a good man and he was good to me in the sense of giving me the material things I thought I needed. I was content. But my misery was obvious. He would prescribe antidepressants for me, but they only took off the edge. After three years into the relationship, I realized I had no life of my own. It was all his. Tom controlled it all.

He told me how to dress, how to act, and what to say. He wanted me to keep up with his image and I was miserable. I didn't know what to do. It took awhile before I got up the nerve to spill my guts and tell Tom I couldn't do this any longer. We remained good friends and he let me stay in one of his houses until I could decide what to do. He was there for me as a friend until the end.

After many years with my partner Tom, our homosexual relationship came to an end. I was completely devastated. I truly loved this man. It wasn't just about the sex. It was the intimacy that two people shared, knowing and caring for one another. It was real. But deep down, I was unsettled and still felt guilty and empty.

So many times I asked God to take away my lust for men. But He wouldn't. I had been hooked on antidepressants off and on for 20 years, and I was trying to get myself clean. I craved men, but when I was with them I was depressed, unfulfilled. So I would take the antidepressants, which was only a temporary fix for the symptoms of my problems, and not the root cause.

By the time I was 39, I had become the successful vice-president of a company in Dallas. I was consuming everyone and everything as I searched for intimacy in my life. I longed for purpose. Sex, money, drugs and alcohol—none of it was enough to fill the void. I fought it tooth and nail. I begged God over and over to take it away. I would be clean for a week, and then by the weekend I would be back on the scene, indulging and wasted on whatever I could get. I became very angry at God. I would scream at Him, but there was only silence in return. Sometimes the silence was deafening. Eventually I refused to even say His name. I sensed that my world was about to crumble, and so, I did what I had done in the past to solve my emptiness; I ran. This time it was to Cozumel, Mexico where I had vacationed many times.

Cozumel had not experienced a hurricane in many years. In 2005, they suffered two in less than eight months—one had hit the day before I was supposed to leave; the other seven months later which was recorded as the largest hurricane in over 100 years. This would foreshadow the dark times in store for me there. Due to my heavy drug and alcohol use, and the darkness and depravity of my mind, I fell out of touch with reality. I was talking to people who didn't exist; physically running from the enemy who was pursuing me in my mind and spirit. I spiraled completely out of control.

My family knew that something was very wrong with me but, due to the hurricane, they could not come to me. I wasn't mentally capable of carrying on a coherent conversation, let alone get myself back to the United States. I was a mental, physical and spiritual train wreck! My best friend, Mikey, was afraid I would end up either dead or in a Mexican prison so he, with the help of his brother-in-law, Gabriel, drove me to the border of the United States. It wasn't until a year later that I recognized the significance of the names Michael and Gabriel (God's Angels).

I returned home depleted but I needed a job. I had blown

through my entire life savings and couldn't think clearly enough to write my name, let alone compose a résumé. I felt totally alienated and completely hopeless. I thought that dying was the only answer to my situation.

In April 2006, I attempted once again to take my own life. I tried to overdose on Xanax. It was then that my family discovered how bad things really were. I had no insurance and no money. They knew I needed more help than they could give me, so they persuaded me to check myself into a reputable mental health facility.

After 36 hours of evaluation the doctors said that they were not equipped to handle someone like me. They gave me one phone call (I called my mom), and then they put me on the front steps until my mom and my brother Ronnie came and picked me up. The look on their faces when they saw me was something I would not soon forget. Feelings of defeat, exhaustion and disappointment covered them. They couldn't believe that the doctors let me out.

I stayed with my mom while I recovered. My Aunt Linda came over often to check on me and to pray over me as would Pastor Jim, who was the pastor at my mom and Linda's church. In retrospect, I realized that our all-knowing God knew those doctors could not give me what I truly needed—a personal relationship with Jesus Christ.

Four weeks later, I felt strong enough to move out from under my mother's care. I found a house about four blocks from hers, and I moved in with bold determination thinking, "I can do this!" It wasn't but two weeks later that I was high again, and this time

I fell hard. Pastor Jim and Aunt Linda met with me and told me about a Christian addiction recovery center in the scenic pine barrens of New Jersey called the Colony of Mercy at America's Keswick.

The Colony of Mercy is a 120-day residential program where, for $150, a man could be freed from the bondage of life-dominating addiction. I didn't want to go there because I believed, as a Christian Ministry, that they would tell me I was going to burn in hell for my homosexual lifestyle. I knew I needed help with my drug and alcohol addiction, but I truly thought that, as far as my homosexuality was concerned, I was still okay in the eyes of God. For me, homosexuality was not negotiable. This was who I was, like it or not. But when I began looking realistically at my situation, I knew I was out of options. God had not revealed to me any other opened doors. I filled out an application and began the long wait for a bed to open up at the Christian recovery center.

One summer morning in July 2006, after getting out of the shower and wanting to die, I looked in the mirror and saw deep darkness looking back at me. My eyes reflected an emptiness and hopelessness I had not noticed before. I always felt empty and hopeless on the inside, but I wasn't aware that it showed on the outside. Aunt Linda had come by to take me to coffee that morning. The moment I saw her face, I broke down.

"I don't think I can make it until they call me to come to the Colony," I sobbed. She barely got through the doorway before she gathered me in her arms. I must have looked a sight. As I cried on her shoulder, she whispered, "Billy, what you need to have is a grateful heart. That's what will get you through until they call." I pulled back and looked into her eyes. Before I even realized I was talking, the words poured out, "Linda, I do not have one thing in my life to be grateful for." Sadly, I meant every word.

Later that night, I was lying in my bed. I had the TV on in the background for noise because I couldn't stand to be alone; the silence constantly reminding me who I was and who I will forever be. The channel was random. The message was not. A lady came on saying, "If you aren't sure of your salvation, grab your Bible and turn with me to Romans chapter 10." I leaped out of bed and began to read along with her. At that moment, on my knees, I asked God to send Jesus into my life to take over the horrible mess I had made of it. Torrents of tears streamed down my face and I was sweating and praying with all my heart.

Suddenly I cried out, "Thank You, Jesus, for my mother. Thank You, for my aunt. Thank You, for Pastor Jim. And thank You, Lord, for the Christian recovery center that You guided me to." I even thanked Him for the bagel that was sitting on the top of the dresser. For the first time I began to hear God's voice as He spoke to my heart. I could feel His presence and I knew with all certainty that He was real. For the first time in a very long time, I had hope.

That night God put on my heart the desire to serve Him. This was when I asked for Him to remove the idols in my life; everything I craved more than Him. The only thing I had ever wanted to be was a Special Education teacher, so I asked God to help me do something with my life that would enable me to help other people. My Heavenly Father told me that same night, the night of my salvation, that what I was going through with drugs, alcohol and homosexuality *was* the Special Education He wanted me teaching about. I really had no idea what all this meant, but I answered, "Okay, God. I hear you." I knew He had spoken directly to my heart.

The next morning I received a call from the Colony of Mercy telling me that they had a bed available for me. It was supposed to be a 16-week wait, but it had only been two weeks. God was in control. I arrived at the Colony unsure of what to expect but ready to defend my lifestyle. I told Jim, my counselor, that I was only there to be freed from drugs. I made it clear to him that any discussion of homosexuality was off limits. I was very sure that God and I were still okay in this regard.

Later Jim told me that I was the most deceived person he had ever met. He wanted to begin showing me the scriptures about the sin of homosexuality, but he clearly heard God's voice speaking to his heart saying, "I've got this, Jim."

With all the restraint he could gather, Jim asked me only if I would agree to read my Bible. "I came to the Colony to draw closer to God, and I will gladly read my Bible to learn what God has for my life," I told him honestly. I thought for certain I saw relief in Jim's eyes.

Over the next few of months, it seemed that every time I opened my Bible, God was putting verses in front of me regarding sexual immorality and homosexuality. He showed me how He intended men to be with women. I had told God that I wanted to give Him everything, that I wanted to serve Him, and that I would do all that He asked. I just never expected Him to ask for the homosexuality too. It was just too much.

As the cravings continued, I began pacing the halls at night crying out, "Dear God, I cannot do what You're asking me to do." God replied, "I know you can't, Son, but I can if you will just give it to Me." I told Him, "God, You had better be as big as You say You are because I know me, and if I have to do this, it won't happen." I couldn't fathom how God would work in this area of my life, but I knew that He was asking me to lay it down. And so I did. I gave Him my all.

That was almost ten years ago. Since then there have been many times of temptation and struggle. God did not take away my attraction to men. He showed me that because of His love for me and my love for Him that I can choose Him over sin, even when it looked good. There have even been times I had to remind Him that He said He would do this for me. It was when I was the most weak. This is when I would turn to His word and rely on Hebrews 4:14-16. "Therefore, since we have a great high priest who has gone through the heavens, Jesus the Son of God, let us hold firmly to the faith we profess. For we do not have a high priest who is unable to sympathize with our weaknesses, but we have one who has been tempted in every way, just as we are – yet was without sin. Let us then approach the throne of grace with confidence, so that we may receive mercy and find grace to help us in our time of need."

Throughout this process, God continued to show up faithfully in my time of need. He reminded me that in my weakness, His strength was made perfect. Day by day He walked me out of homosexuality. People would ask, "So are you an ex-homosexual?" I would look at them and say, "No! I am a child of the Most High. I am a man of God."

Today, I have joy and peace that cannot be described by anything other than Jesus Christ. I do not need drugs, sex, men or money to complete me. Today, my identity is in Jesus. He has filled the hole in my heart. He has given me a heart of flesh that wills and desires to be obedient to His Word. I know His purpose in my life. I have seen His plan. I have the intimacy I have always yearned for.

My purpose today is to serve my King and allow Him to use me to bring glory to His name. He has restored my mind and my life. The fact that I can write this for you today is a miracle. It was powerful that He delivered me from drugs and alcohol. But the miracle is that He convinced me His Word is true from cover to cover—even the parts about homosexuality. I have not been depressed or needed medication since.

However, in my humanness, there are still times that I grieve the loss of homosexuality; it was like my best friend had died, and I wanted someone in my life. I spent a lot of time looking for the person I thought I was supposed to be with, but all this time it was Jesus. He filled that void inside of me. He gave me a new past, a new present, and a glorious new future. God is so gracious and so very patient, and I am more blessed than I can say.

After I graduated from the Colony of Mercy, I stayed on and served as the Director of Development. I worked hard and I learned so much about our Lord. When an opening for Colony Chaplin came up, I put in for it and was blessed with the position. For five years I served God as a fulltime Chaplain at the Colony. This call from God allowed me to share the hope that I have found in Jesus Christ with other men trapped in the bondage of addiction and sin. I lived it and God knew that He could use my life's choices to help others through their challenges and defeat their demons. Our Lord will never let a tear go to waste, and He can always turn what is meant for evil into good, if we want it bad enough, and if we put our trust in Him fully.

Over time, God gave me a beautiful, healthy desire for women and to have a wife one day. The most amazing of all is that God has given me the desire for children. This was a real surprise, for never in my most surreal moments did I ever think to want a child of my own. But as I look to my God, I know that even this is possible. I hope to have a son one day who will carry on my family name.

God is amazing! He has changed my life, my heart and my desires. I am excited to see how He will continue to change me and use me over the upcoming days, months and years. God can change anyone who believes, even the homosexual.

Hope, Healing and Wholeness for the Homosexual

For the first half of my life I was torn by the conflict going on inside of me. My church and family felt that homosexuality was wrong. The world was indifferent and I couldn't seem to control my same sex attractions no matter how hard I tried. I didn't wake up one day thinking I will sleep with men. It was something that happened at such an early age; it seemed as if I was born this way. The truth is I had no control over the desires. What I didn't realize then was that I could choose how I would respond to those desires.

Trying to change the desires in my own strength led to many failed promises, and I often said to myself, "I will never do that again." But I always did; then came the depression and thoughts of suicide. I started attending a church where they claimed that God was okay with homosexuality; in fact, they stated that God made me gay. I was looking for an answer and I liked that one. Fortunately for me, the story doesn't end there.

The truth is I never studied the scriptures for myself. While I did have some fun times (Hebrews 11:25 "…sin is pleasurable for a season…"), and good friends in the gay community, it was never enough to fill the hole in my heart. I was always searching for something or someone new in an effort to fill myself. I was worshipping everything except the One true God, and I was trading the truth about God for a lie (Romans 1:21-32). It was a lie that fit my situation; however the real truth is that "the wages of sin is death" (Romans 6:23).

True intimacy and sex as God intended can only be found between a husband and a wife. God intended sex to be good. He created sex and told Adam and Eve to be fruitful and multiply. It is a spiritual act of worship that brings glory to God as a husband and wife become one in the flesh. Because we live in a fallen world, sex has become corrupted and our desires have run amok. The good news is that God has a plan to redeem our fallen state through His Son, Jesus Christ!

"For God so loved the world, that he gave his only Son, that whoever believes in him should not perish but have eternal life" (John 3:16).

I wasn't capable of changing in my own strength; however, once I had accepted Jesus as my Lord and Savior, God began to convince me that His word was true from cover to cover. Not just in the parts I chose to read and obey, but everywhere in the Bible. When God is in the picture, all things are possible! Matthew 19:26, But Jesus looked at them and said, "With man this is impossible, but with God all things are possible."

God can change anyone, even a man like me who has spent most of his life in relationships with other men—a man trapped in sexual addictions, pornography and drug use. And He can change you too! His word says in Romans 1:16, "For I am not ashamed of the gospel, for it is the power of God for salvation to everyone who believes, to the Jew first and also to the Greek."

In Matthew 11:28, Jesus tells us, "Come to me, all who labor and are heavy laden, and I will give you rest." It's true! You can have an abundant life full of joy and peace. Jesus can set you free from the bondage of sin.

The first and most important step to walking away from homosexuality and living the life God intends for you is having Jesus Christ as your Lord and Savior. This is the only way to Heaven, and I believe to lasting freedom over same sex attraction and homosexuality.

Romans 10:9 "…because, if you confess with your mouth that

Jesus is Lord and believe in your heart that God raised him from the dead, you will be saved."

This is where our hope begins:
A) Admit that you are a sinner.
B) Believe that Jesus died on the cross to save you from your sins.
C) Confess that He is your Lord and Savior.

Did you know that Jesus has been helping people walk away from homosexuality for over 2,000 years? We can see this clearly in 1Corinthians 6:9-11 "…Or do you not know that the unrighteous will not inherit the kingdom of God? Do not be deceived: neither the sexually immoral, nor idolaters, nor adulterers, nor men who practice homosexuality, nor thieves, nor the greedy, nor drunkards, nor revilers, nor swindlers will inherit the kingdom of God. And such were some of you. ***But you were washed, you were sanctified, you were justified in the name of the Lord Jesus Christ and by the Spirit of our God."***

The Bible doesn't tell us that God will automatically take away our temptation or that there will not be struggles. In fact, it tells us the opposite.

John 16:33 says "…In the world you will have tribulation. But take heart; I have overcome the world."

1Corinthians 10:13: "No temptation has overtaken you that is not common to man. God is faithful, and he will not let you be tempted beyond your ability, but with the temptation he will also provide the way of escape, that you may be able to endure it."

The world would like for us to believe that we should participate in anything that feels good to us. In fact, over the years, people all over the world stand in celebration of "coming out" and being courageous, admitting that they are homosexual, and proud of it. But they have it all wrong. It is not a celebration, it is fornication, as the Bible clearly states. God's Commandments are meant to protect us. He has a plan for our lives better than anything we could plan for ourselves; however, it depends on us being obedient to His word, even when it goes against what feels natural to us.

Matthew 16:24: Then Jesus told his disciples, "If anyone would come after me, let him deny himself and take up his cross and follow me."

Jeremiah 29:11: "For I know the plans I have for you," declares the LORD, "plans to prosper you and not to harm you, to give you hope and a future."

It is important to understand that we are weak, and in our own strength we will give into temptations. Did you know that Jesus was tempted in every way just as you are? He can understand your pain and asks you to cry out to Him when you are weak.

Hebrews 4:15-16: "For we do not have a high priest who is unable to sympathize with our weaknesses, but one who in every respect has been tempted as we are, yet without sin. Let us then with confidence draw near to the throne of grace, that we may receive mercy and find grace to help in time of need."

2Corinthians 12:9-10: "But he said to me, 'My grace is sufficient for you, for my power is made perfect in weakness.' Therefore I will boast all the more gladly of my weaknesses, so that the power of Christ may rest upon me. For the sake of Christ, then, I am content with weaknesses, insults, hardships, persecutions, and calamities. For when I am weak, then I am strong."

God may not completely take away same sex attractions. Our pursuit should be to live a holy life that is pleasing to God. 1Peter 1:16 says, "You shall be holy, for I am holy." Set reasonable expectations and ask God to change your heart. Then, "Delight yourself in the LORD, and he will give you the desires of your heart. Commit your way to the LORD; trust in him, and he will act" (Psalm 37:4-5).

Don't give up on yourself, or on God. He has a plan and it is perfect. He will renew your mind and give you His perspective as you give your life to Him. This comes through structured Bible reading, devotions (alone time with God), prayer and fellowship with the body of Christ. "Ah Sovereign Lord, you have made the heavens and the earth by your great power and out-stretched hand. Nothing is too hard or too wonderful for You" (Jeremiah 32:17).

2Corinthians 5:17: "Therefore, if anyone is in Christ, he is a new creation. The old has passed away; behold, the new has come."

In the summer of 2014, the Lord began stirring my heart once again. God was clearly telling me to leave Keswick and set up camp in South West Philadelphia and start a new ministry. I didn't want to leave the Colony. I loved my ministry. I told my friends, "I don't know what God is doing. But there is no mistaking His call." So after eight years, I gave my notice as the Colony Chaplain and left Keswick in October 2014. I went to Philadelphia, following the Voice of God once again.

Shortly after, New Hope Philly was born. It has become my passion. New Hope Philly is a discipleship ministry for men who have come out of life-dominating sins. These men are being trained to become ministers and missionaries in South West Philadelphia. Who better than I could do this for Christ, for I have already been where these men are going? It is my joy to serve my God in such a way, at such a time as this.

If you have any questions for Pastor Bill, or you would like to donate to his new cause for Christ, go to www.newhopephilly.com. Your emails are most welcomed.

"For I will take you out of the nations; I will gather you from all the countries and bring you back into your own land. I will sprinkle clean water on you, and you will be clean; I will cleanse you from all your impurities and from all your idols. I will give you a new heart and put a new spirit in you; I will remove from you your heart of stone and give you a heart of flesh. And I will put my Spirit in you and move you to follow my decrees and be careful to keep my laws. You will live in the land I gave your forefathers; you will be my people, and I will be your God" (Ezekiel 36:24-28.)

Innocence Shattered - Life Renewed

This isn't an easy story to tell but I know it's the right thing to do. It is the most tragic heartbreak of my life. After you read how I was raised and the choices that my family and I made, you will witness an innocent life shattered beyond repair and another life forever renewed—but only by the grace of God.

To be able to say that my parents are still married is something you don't hear very often these days. To my knowledge they never fought or, at least, never in front of me. There were many siblings in our household: An older brother, Peter, a younger brother Andrew, and five half sisters, who were already grown, married and having kids of their own by the time I was born. So even though I have a lot of sisters, I grew up as a middle child, and the only girl.

My mom and dad decided early on not to raise us as Christians. My dad grew up Seventh-Day-Adventist, but is agnostic. My mom grew up Catholic, but doesn't practice. They would sometimes take us to church on holidays or when we visited relatives. We thought it boring and couldn't wait for it to end.

My grandmother on my dad's side was a very strong Christian. When we visited, she would play on the piano "Jesus Loves Me" and other hymns, until her eyes got bad and her hands no longer worked. I never learned to play the piano, and right now we don't have room for it, but that piano is mine, and I hope that someday my kids and I will learn to play it together.

Gramma was the one who taught us who Jesus is. My brothers would sleep in the living room, and I would always sleep with Gramma. I'd lay there and listen to her talk to Jesus as if He were right there in the room. She loved the Lord with all her heart. I am so grateful to her, because without her I would have never heard about Him. I never forgot the Jesus she told me about. Through all my shyness and rebellion, abuse and depression, crushing grief and guilt, and even joy and happiness, I never forgot Him—even when I ignored the fact that He existed at all.

For as long as I can remember, my parents deliberately worked split shifts in order to avoid the costs of childcare. Sometimes when they were both gone, they left my older brother Peter in charge. When I think of Peter, the single most descriptive word that comes to mind is cruel—he was cruel to the bone.

Peter was mean and uncaring. He cheated at every game. If I argued, I got ridiculed or beaten, but sometimes we were silly and had fun. Yet I still had to be on guard constantly for it could turn in an instant! I had to be careful of everything I said and did. I was torn between hating my brother and wanting to do everything right to gain his approval.

However, when Peter got into Dungeons and Dragons (a role playing video game with different characters), things became increasingly worse. He was in the 5th grade at the time and failing every class. My parents were told by the hobby-shop salesman that this game would help him with his reading and math. They thought they were doing the right thing for their son when they bought it for him. But very soon after, Peter would hold up in his room for hours and play fantasy games for days on end. It was only a matter of time before the lines between fantasy and reality began to blur his vision.

Peter became so strange that he started saving his own blood in vials, vials which he found in my grandpa's old medical bag. My brother would make strange concoctions with his blood that he would boil up at night. He called it his wine. Then he would drink it. Sometimes he would even dare me to drink it. Sadly I did. I knew that if I didn't, he would, at best, verbally abuse me. At worst, he would beat, bite or scratch me. I wanted so desperately not to be afraid of him, so most of the time I did it to prove that I wasn't scared—but inside I was scared to death.

The biting and beating was bad enough, but it wasn't the worst part. Peter would often bare his teeth in a snarl like an animal and would grab me by the neck and shove me up against the wall. Then he would dig his fingernails into my body and squeeze as hard as he could until he saw fear in my eyes. He would actually file his fingernails and toenails into points like claws, so they would be as sharp as nails.

Whenever he went barefoot (which he did a lot), his toenails would make clicking sounds on the sidewalk. In fact, he would often run on all fours, doing it as fast, or even faster than he'd run on two. When my younger brother Andrew got old enough, he started getting the brunt of all Peter's anger and cruelty. Poor Andrew was picked on relentlessly, but he refused to back down. It broke my heart when I watched my little brother get beaten up all the time, though I could do little to ease his fear and pain.

I am so embarrassed to admit that there was also some "sex play" that went on between Peter and me. I was four years younger and wasn't sure how much of it was normal until a dear friend loved me enough to tell me the truth: It was abuse, and it was sin. We also had a male neighbor friend who was my age, living next door with his grandparents because his mom had a drug problem. Sex play was all he ever wanted to do and, sadly, I wasn't much better. He wasn't mean like Peter. He was just weird and an outcast. I later learned that he had been molested by his stepfather.

My preoccupation with all of this added to many of my problems in school. I was very much to myself, afraid to say the wrong thing. Most of the time, I said nothing at all. That defense only caused more ridicule and isolation. I was so lonely.

When I reached puberty, Peter finally stopped being cruel to me. In fact, he became almost sickeningly affectionate, although the sex play had stopped long before. The worst was when he wanted to talk to me about his fantasies, which were by then realities to him. I hated listening to him talk about the evil characters he made up and who he wished he was. When I tried to leave he would look at me sadly and ask, "Don't you want to hear how it ends, Val?" But it never did end! He was 18 years old and still playing Dungeons and Dragons, pretending to be living out his life as a werewolf or a vampire. It was sad. It was weird. And it was so very scary. The few friends I had made thought it was funny, but they got to go home at the end of the day. Unfortunately for me, I was already home.

When I was 15, Peter joined the Army. I felt free at last! This was around the time that boys started to notice me. I had my first boyfriend, my first broken heart, and my first teenage obsession. Then, I met Oscar. He was my first real love. Once we finally got together, it was me who had to convince him to be intimate, which took at least three months. I remember him telling me, "But Val, don't you understand, if we do 'that', I would just be using you?" And I was like, "Phishaw! No you wouldn't. I know you love me." I was just 17 when he finally gave into my pleas.

Two years later it felt as if my world collapsed when I learned that Oscar had cheated on me. What little self-esteem I had left was completely obliterated. I didn't feel that my self-worth or my body was worth saving for anyone anymore. This was when I started drinking and smoking weed. It was also when I became interested in the occult, listening to dark music, and experimenting with New Age spirituality and Wicca (witchcraft), which I had already been introduced to by my older brother. Although I didn't attend church nor was I reading the Bible at the time, I felt the Lord was with me, even through this period in my life of confusion and destructive choices. I still found myself talking to Him because I never felt like anything or anyone else ever heard me.

By this time I had another boyfriend, but I still wasn't happy. It didn't take long before I began to spiral out of control. I was at a party one night and got really drunk. The entire evening was a blur and I only recall bits and pieces. But then something horrible happened. I was in a group with several guys and vaguely remember them coming onto me. Afterwards, I claimed rape and I felt raped. I was too intoxicated to fight them off and they took advantage of me. After a frantic phone call home, Peter (who had just gotten home from the army), and his girlfriend Roberta picked me up and drove me to the hospital. After being examined and interviewed, I was informed that I could not press charges because I did not tell them "No!" When my parents showed up to take me home, I was mortified. It was the most humiliating thing I had ever been through. No charges were ever filed. There wasn't enough evidence. But I know the truth—and so do they.

During this time Roberta and I had become very close. She was only 17 and I always wondered what she saw in Peter. I felt sorry for her being stuck in his role playing world. But it was her choice. She had rejected her Christian roots long before she met him, which made it easier for him to pull her down with him, into his evil world of make believe.

I remember when Peter broke the news that Roberta was

having a baby. He claimed that they had done a "fertility spell" and now she was pregnant. Roberta asked naively, "Do you think Peter will be a good dad?" I felt sick to my stomach, because I knew in my brother's current state of mind he wouldn't be good for anything or anyone. "Of course he will," I told her. What else could I say?

After much thought, I chose not to tell my current boyfriend about my horrible incident at the party. Instead of facing the consequences of my actions, I ran away. I went to Seattle to study art. Within the first few months I was there, I got involved with the lead singer in a Goth/Grunge band. His name was Brock. He informed me that he had a live-in girlfriend but that he still wanted to see me. I thought his invitation to meet him at the studio at one o'clock in the morning was odd, but I still went.

Eventually our early morning rendezvous turned into a once-a-week ordeal. I had to walk through downtown Seattle in the middle of the night by myself to meet this guy, who refused to leave his girlfriend because she supported him. I know God was with me there, also. If He hadn't been, I would have surely been dead and lying in a gutter somewhere.

After several more months, I grew disillusioned; Brock and I broke up and art school ended up not being what I thought it would be. I didn't want to design logos and labels; I wanted to make art. I dropped out after two semesters. Everything in Seattle got to the point where I couldn't stand being there anymore; the drinking, the drugs, the dreariness, the bad relationships, and the failures. I called Oscar sobbing hysterically. I felt as if he was the only one, besides my parents, who had ever loved me for me. I wanted to go home. Oscar was waiting for me when I got back.

While I was still in Seattle, Peter and Roberta had gotten married and were living with my parents. A short time later, little Kelly was born. She was six months old when Oscar and I moved in. Kelly's crib was in our bedroom, so we became the default carriers in the middle of the night. Many times I would pound on the wall for them to come take care of their daughter. Some days Kelly would not stop crying. She didn't want me. She wanted her mom. But more often than not it was my mom who came to the rescue.

Eventually, my dad moved the crib into their room. His hope was that it would force my brother and his wife to pay more attention to their daughter. When Roberta discovered what my dad had done, she ran out of the house crying. Looking back, I wish my dad had kept the crib in my room.

There were nine people living in the house at the time: Oscar and me, Andrew and his girlfriend, Peter, Roberta, Kelly, and my mom and dad. Peter and Roberta spent most of their time at home in the sunroom, which they had taken over as their fantasy game room. They would be out there for hours, chain smoking and pretending to be people they weren't. Yes, my brother had finally convinced Roberta to be just like him. Kelly would pound on the glass crying for attention, or they would leave her in her car seat on the floor or in her high chair for hours on end. Every night they would ask one of us if we would watch her so that they could meet their role playing, pagan friends at Denny's. It got to the point that if my parents were home sleeping and no one else was there, my brother and his wife would just put Kelly to bed around 5:30pm, lock their bedroom door and leave. No one else had a key but them.

Finally my parents told them both they needed to take responsibility for their daughter and not be out all night. They said they would take care of it, but they never did. There were times when I would come home to the sounds of her crying behind the locked door while my mom and dad slept. Several times Andrew would pick the lock so we could get her out. But when Andrew wasn't around, I would lie down in front of the door and play with her. She could see one of my eyes through the keyhole and I could see hers. I think just seeing a small part of me and hearing my voice made her feel less lonely. It also stopped her from crying... for a while. Andrew, his girlfriend, Oscar and I used to talk about calling Child Protective Service, but we didn't want Kelly to be taken away from us, and we didn't trust the foster care system. We just wanted my brother and Roberta to pay more attention to their daughter...but they never did.

It was my mom who usually received the brunt of everything. Every moment she wasn't working or sleeping, she was taking care of her "little sunshine". She loved that baby with all her heart, but the rest of us (me included) were breaking her heart: Peter and Roberta by resenting and ignoring parenthood; I, by being intimate with Oscar before marriage under her own roof; my dad by smoking weed; and everyone else by disrespecting and taking advantage of her. I actually think she was oblivious to most of it because she was always so busy cooking and cleaning for nine people who ignored her needs and helped very little with anything.

Kelly was two when her mother walked out. Roberta decided she no longer wanted to be married to my brother, and she hated being a mom. Peter was devastated—and I was devastated for Kelly. With Peter being her only parent left, this little girl didn't stand much of a chance for any type of normal childhood.

When I was 20 years old I found out that I was pregnant. I was nowhere near ready to be a mom but I already loved the life that was growing inside me. When I shared my news with Oscar, I thought he'd feel the same, but I was wrong; he was furious. He demanded that I have an abortion. After the appointment had been made he let me know in no uncertain terms that, "If you have this baby, Val, I won't be there. I don't know how to be a father. I swear I will leave you and never come back! Do you want your baby to be like Kelly? Do you want to do this to your parents? Because they are the ones who are going to have to take care of it! I won't do it, Val. I just can't!"

Oscar's sister had married a Christian man, and I begged him to talk to Oscar. He tried, but Oscar wouldn't listen. The next day I was completely numb. I was so lethargic I could barely walk. I didn't want to go. Oscar had to carry me to the car. I sobbed silently all the way. I prayed to God that we would crash so that I wouldn't have to do what I was about to do. When I was lying on the table, I remember looking away from the ultrasound as I drifted off into oblivion. I just couldn't watch as this tiny life was being taken from me.

The next day I was still living in a nightmare. I was cramping and bleeding, and my milk came in. No one ever told me about this part. There was no baby! Why would I have milk? Oscar thought it was funny. I was devastated and inconsolable. That milk was reality to me. It was meant to feed and nourish my baby. But I had no baby! I was so angry and so hurt by what he made me do. I could barely look at him. I vowed then and there to never, ever choose a man over my child again!

It didn't take long before our relationship crumbled and we parted ways. I was still so distraught over losing my baby, I reached out to Brock (remember him from Seattle?). He seemed so sincere and always said the right thing; and he gave me the attention and sympathy I needed. When he asked me to move to Los Angeles with him, how could I refuse? Saying goodbye to Kelly was the hardest thing I had to do. Brock wooed me until he got me away from my family.

It wasn't long before he started telling me how to dress, how to wear my hair and makeup, how to walk, how to talk, who I should and shouldn't talk to, and what I could and couldn't say to them. He would grope me in public, and our intimacy was very frequent and always violent.

Brock also felt the need to put me on a very strict diet. I was allowed six grams of fat a day. If I wore any clothes around the apartment it meant that I did not love him. So I complied wearing nothing but a half-hearted smile. I was there almost a year before a friend began to recognize the signs. I was forever grateful when she came and rescued me.

I spent the next few months back at my parents' house, playing with Kelly, hiking the hills with friends or just by myself, and going up to Lake Tahoe and climbing on the rocks, which was my passion. I listened to Reggae music and went to shows. I felt alive and free for the first time in a very long time. This was in 2000.

I met Tino in September of that same year. He was wonderful to me. And we both had a deep love for Reggae (Jamaican-style music). He knew and understood Reggae like no one else. After our third date, we were walking back to the car and he just blurted out, "I love you Val. I... I mean, I know I'm not supposed to say that yet, but I do. I love you." I found great comfort in his words. He seemed so very sincere.

Life moved on and was about as good as it could get until my brother Peter announced that he was moving to New York… and taking Kelly with him! We were aware that he had met a fellow Wiccan online, but we had no idea it had gotten serious. Her name was Tabitha. She was a nurse and was 17 years his senior. Peter informed us that he was packing up his four-year-old daughter and going back east to live with this woman. We were shocked. We thought for sure he'd leave Kelly behind and that my parents would eventually get custody. I was beyond scared for her. I knew Kelly's life would be challenging, but nothing could have prepared any of us for the road that lay ahead. I was kissing her goodbye when she turned to my dad and said, "Take good care of her, okay?" Her concern for me was heartwarming, yet so sad at the same time.

Soon after, I moved in with Tino in South Shores, Lake Tahoe. We smoked pot and cigarettes all day, every day, and we drank and had barbecues every weekend. I was working at a gym less than a block away and walked through the woods to get there. It was so amazing. It felt like heaven. When I was home, I would make art while Tino practiced his Hip Hop sets. I remember standing at the counter one day carving a lion pipe when he looked at me and said, "I'm going to marry you someday." I smiled and hoped it would be true. I knew God had blessed me greatly by bringing me to the mountains, among the trees and the blue waters of Lake Tahoe and giving me Tino. I was truly happy.

Three months into our relationship I found out I was pregnant. I was so scared. So was Tino. He knew what I had gone through before. I told him I would leave if he wanted me to, and that he didn't have to take any responsibility whatsoever. I would never ask him for anything, but I was having this baby no matter what! He proposed on December 31st. We married on March 10, 2001.

Marriage was hard for me and because my sense of worth had always been tied to my physical beauty and attractiveness, pregnancy was hard for me too. Tino struggled through it as well. He was laid off work several times but would always find another job within a week or two. Still it was so stressful on both of us. Tino had never wanted to bring children into this world, at least not until he had the security of constant and dependable employment. Sometimes, however, the most cherished blessings happen when you least expect them.

By the time our precious daughter was born that August, it

didn't matter what we used to think. The moment she cried, we looked at each other, and we knew our lives had forever changed. The nurse brought our daughter to me, and she looked right at me like she knew who I was. She was the most beautiful thing I had ever seen. We named her Jamie.

We moved when Jamie was three months old. I never wanted to leave Tahoe (and deep down I resented the move). We were completely unprepared for what childcare would cost, so I convinced Tino that I should be a stay-at-home mom. It turns out that I wasn't very good at it. I didn't want to cook and clean and take care of a baby all day by myself. We lived in a cute, but extremely tiny little shack, barely big enough for one, let alone three. Tino would come home in a bad mood and we'd fight. Soon, our heaven had turned into hell and we were miserable.

In our second year of marriage we separated. I took our baby and went home to my parents. I didn't want to be divorced, but I didn't want to be married either. I didn't want to be a single mother, and I certainly didn't want to live with my parents again. I had no job, no childcare, no education. I was lost. I decided to go back to school.

One day over the phone Tino told me he missed us and wanted us to come home. As soon as the semester was over, I transferred my classes to be closer to him, and Jamie and I went home. I was in my fourth semester at school, and had also been doing a federal work study program that paid for childcare (with about $50 a month left over) when I found out I was pregnant again. Tino was not happy, and although I didn't know how I could keep going to school and pay for two kids in childcare, I would not consider abortion. I couldn't. That's when I signed up for an online school that offered associate degrees. We went into debt, but I was able to stay home and do my classes. I kept my grades up too.

After my beautiful little Lilly was born that September, I had an IUD put in so that I would be protected for ten years. When she was six months old, I had a hard time keeping up on my classes. My face started breaking out, and I had missed my cycle. We were struggling to survive on the $9 an hour Tino was making when I found out I was pregnant again! It wasn't fair!

When I went for my first check up, I learned that the IUD had been put in wrong. It had worked its way in between my uterus and intestines, encased in body tissue and the tissue had formed around it. Thankfully it wasn't a threat to the baby, but Tino was still worried out of his mind nearly to the state of panic. He begged me to get an abortion. But I just couldn't do it. I found myself praying often during this pregnancy, that I could deliver a healthy baby and that everything would be okay. I also begged God to give me a boy so that Tino might be happier about us having another child, and that he would finally have a son.

I tried to keep my mind off our situation and began focusing on my niece Kelly. She was still living in New York with my brother and his new wife Tabitha, the same one he had met online. The horror stories I would hear from my mom were frightening and my heart grieved for Kelly who was only six at the time. When Kelly got into trouble, one of her punishments was having her phone privileges taken away, which meant she wasn't allowed to talk to us.

Poor Kelly was locked in her room every evening at 5:00pm, and was made to wear an alarm that would go off whenever she got out of bed. On rare occasions when we were able to actually speak to Kelly, her personality would change drastically if her stepmother walked in on our conversation. She'd go from chattering and laughter to one word answers. My mom went to visit a few times and said that she would take Kelly to a hotel because the house was so disgusting and it reeked of cat urine.

My Aunt Sharon also went to visit once. She said it was the worst living conditions she had ever seen, and it stunk so bad that you could hardly breathe. There where cats and kittens in every room, and a few chickens too. Stacks of dirty dishes were in the kitchen sink and on the counters and there were piles of laundry everywhere. It was obvious that no one ever cleaned up after themselves. Kelly was forced to wash her own clothes in the bathtub with only a small bar of soap and a plunger. But washing never seemed to help. The smell of urine permeated everything she owned, even her backpack that she took to school.

My aunt tried to talk to Peter a few times, but he ignored her pleas. Still she felt she had to try because she only had this one chance to help save this child. Aunt Sharon was dying of cancer. She didn't have much time left. She was also very troubled that Peter's wife's mentally challenged adult son, Alan was living with them. My aunt let me know in no uncertain terms that she did not trust Alan around Kelly. That's when she told me I should do something because I was the only one who might be strong enough. The neighbors agreed. So I called CPS in New York and told them what I knew, but it wasn't enough. They said it seemed extreme but did not constitute abuse. I didn't want Kelly in the foster care system anyway. I didn't want to lose her and yet I knew the squalor she lived in was horrific. But my hands were tied and there was no way to remedy the situation from 3000 miles away. Time passed and Kelly continued to endure the trauma and suffering. Little did we know how truly bad it was until several years later.

When I was five months along, I found out that I was having a boy! I was so excited. I thought Tino would be too. When I brought the ultrasound home to show him, my husband had very little to say. Our sweet Daniel was born by C-section four months later. I managed to push my way through my online classes with a four year old, an 18 month old, and an infant, underfoot—all while recovering from surgery. I was suffering daily with the stress of an unhealthy marriage and neighbors trying to convince me that a degree was a waste of time and money. It was beyond difficult.

In the summer of 2006 (five years later), Kelly finally came to visit. She was nine years old. We all went to the airport to meet her. She was so tiny, but so happy. It looked as if her little feet couldn't keep themselves on the ground as she made her way over to us while squealing the whole time. Jamie ran to meet her as they collided into one another, then collapsing in a giggling heap on the floor in the middle of the airport. It was priceless. As soon as Kelly could get up she ran to me and threw her arms around me like I was the most important person in the world.

We went to the McDonald's play park, and for the first time my kids got to play with their "Cousin Kelly", as she would forever be known to them. She stayed for six weeks, mostly with my mom and dad, but with us, too. Oh, the fun we had! Those six weeks went by so quickly and all too soon it was over. We hated sending her home. She kissed us and hugged us and held on tight. Her stomach ached and her head hurt, but still she wanted to go home. She said she missed her daddy.

After Kelly left, the neighbors started in on their anti-Tino campaign, saying he'd told a mutual friend he had cheated on me. I didn't know what to think. I was crying at the stove making dinner and he was so upset, pleading with me. "Val, I don't blame you for being so upset. If they were saying things like that about you, I'd be going crazy too, but I didn't do it. I would never do that to you, Val. I swear. But if you want me to, I'll leave, and you can be with them, and you can be just like them, because that sounds like what you want! Is that what you want?"

At that moment I saw clearly what those people were really like. They smoked and drank and consumed…They bought useless merchandise to fill up that hole of empty nothingness, yet they were never satisfied. They made a lot of money but lived in a worse shack than ours. They never spoke positively about or to anyone. They were manipulative, angry and two-faced. Why would I think they were being anything but? They had never liked Tino, and I had fed their hatred with my disrespect.

These people shunned God, and even though I hadn't given myself fully to Him because I didn't know what it meant to do so, I heard from Him clear as day: "Don't believe them! Stay with your husband. It's what I want for you!" It was the first time I knew with certainty that I had heard from God. I knew I needed to cut them off. This made me realize that you are who you surround yourself with. I did not want to be "them" anymore, so I cut the ties. Shortly after this, we moved to a quaint little town in the valley where Jamie started kindergarten. Life was moving forward. It wasn't always great and we still fought every day, but at least we were together and trying to make it work.

I graduated that year, but I didn't go back to work. Kelly came back that next summer and we had such a wonderful time together again. We played in the backyard; watched movies over and over; and walked in the "Relay for Life" (a race for victims and survivors of cancer) with Aunt Sharon. The girls had sleepovers at Gramma's house, and she and Tino had some epic pillow fights. The memories we gave her would last us a lifetime. But all too soon it was over.

By summer's end, we were getting ready to say goodbye to Kelly and send her home again. As always, there were hushed conversations about how she would have headaches and stomachaches before she had to leave, and we hoped her stepmom and family were treating her well. Also remembering Aunt Sharon's warning about the stepson Alan, we hoped he wasn't a danger to her. He was awfully weird, but Kelly seemed to like him and never spoke bad about him. In fact, she never said anything negative about any of her family. She said that Alan was always the one who fed her and played games with her. Though he was 27 years old, he had the mind and emotions of a 12-year-old boy. That's probably why they got along so well.

I asked Kelly questions, but nothing directly or specific. I had heard once that you weren't supposed to ask kids leading questions so they would be more likely to tell you what was real instead of what they thought you wanted to hear. I wished I had never heard that. I wished I had asked the hard questions; the ones I didn't want to know the answers to.

In 2008, two days before Kelly was to come back for another six weeks, my dad called. He told me to call Kelly. She was home alone and she didn't want her parents to see the charges on their bill. Kelly was locked in her room when I called her, and she answered on the first ring. While we were on the phone, I read to her as my kids sat and listened. It was almost as if we were all there together in the same room. Before we hung up, we said our prayers. Afterward, Kelly was very reverent and spoke from her heart when she said, "In Jesus' name, amen." It was precious. Yet, I was so very angry at my brother for the conditions my sweet niece had to live in, and for them locking her in her room every day. But I knew that soon she would be with us, so I let it go and never said a word.

Kelly came back that year but with less fire in her spirit, and she seemed to whine and complain about everything, which was not like her at all. She hated the meals I made and never seemed satisfied or content. Tino worked so much he didn't have time for pillow fights. Another thing we all noticed was how she was wearing her hair. She had it styled so that it would hang over one eye, the same eye, every day. When I tried to change it up a bit, she told me, "I can't see out of that eye anyway, so what's the point?"

My mom took her to the eye doctor a few days later, and he informed her that Kelly was blind in that eye. She had been diagnosed with lazy eye when she was an infant and had surgery to correct it when she was two. Peter was supposed to follow up with therapy, but he never did. Blindness was the result. What sadness and pain this poor child had been through in such a short period of time. My heart was constantly breaking for her.

Kelly was 11 years old and had spent that summer doing things she had never done before. She was allowed to have her first sleepover with a friend, and my parents took her to Disneyland for the first time. Kelly had such a wonderful time seeing the sights and having her picture taken with all the Disney characters and riding on all the rides. When she got back, we had a big graduation ceremony for her as she would be going into the 6th grade when she got home to New York. We also walked in the "Relay for Life" race again, but this time without Aunt Sharon. She had passed away a few months before and we all grieved her absence and missed her terribly.

Kelly got sick again with headaches and stomach pains a few days before she had to leave. This time she actually begged us to let her stay. She didn't want to go home. She didn't hug any of us with much enthusiasm when I dropped her off at my parents' house. This bothered me a lot. I was halfway to my car when I realized I wasn't going to settle for a distant unemotional hug from this child whom I adored. I quickly did an about face and ran back inside. When I opened the door, she looked up and I ran to her. I had to have just one more hug. Then I went home and the whispers started again.

We all wanted Kelly to be with us, living with us, and feeling safe and loved. It was obvious that things in New York were horrible, and probably unbearable for her at times, but we also knew she would have to be 12 before she could legally choose in court where she wanted to live. It wouldn't be long. Less than a year. But as it turned out, we didn't even have a month.

Three weeks later, on August 29, 2008, I got a call from my dad. He sobbed into the phone, "Val, Kelly's had an accident! She got something wrapped around her neck and she wasn't breathing. She's being care-flighted to the hospital right now. The paramedics said she might not make it. Mom is on her way home right now. Can you come over? She wants her kids here with her. She's afraid of what she might hear when Peter calls."

I had to wait for Tino to get home, but I immediately grabbed my kids and we all got on our knees and prayed. I begged God for her life! "Lord, please save this child! Please don't let her die! I'll take her, I promise! I'll never let her go back there! She'll be like my own. Please don't take her!"

By the time we got to my parent's house, my brother Andrew was already there. We looked at each other and I knew we were all thinking the same thing—this was not an accident. My mom was rushing around, talking faster than normal, trying to come up with scenarios as to how this could have happened. Was it the boa she'd given her? Was it the beads? She could have been sleeping. Had she tied something too tight?

I was upstairs with Mom when Peter called. She grabbed the phone and I watched as the blood literally drained from her face. Peter told her that Kelly was brain dead. The doctor informed them she wouldn't last through the night. I tried to comfort my grieving mother but she was inconsolable. She threw my hands away screaming into the phone, "NO! Not Kelly. Not Kelly!" I was numb. I could barely move. It wasn't real. It couldn't be.

It was 4am on August 30th when they let her go. I started smoking again that day, and I hit the ganja pipe for the first time since Jamie was a baby, but it just made everything worse. Phones calls were made and received, friends and family were coming and going, and I was on the computer looking for information as to what could have happened, and trying to keep the other side of her family informed as well. Then it came out. A very short article stating that the death of the little girl from upstate New York was being investigated as a homicide.

A short time later, my Dad called. "Val!" he sobbed, "Oh Val, Kelly was raped..." He was crying hysterically. I could barely understand him. "Oh dear God, that poor little girl! Someone raped her!"

I was on my knees. I couldn't get up. Grief and guilt were crushing me, sucking the breath out of me. "We KNEW they didn't treat her right!" I was screaming at him. "We KNEW! And none of us did ANYTHING! We sent her HOME, Dad! We LET her go back there! We... didn't... do... ANYTHING!"

I ended up back at my parents, although I don't know how. I could barely remember moving or speaking or eating. I was underwater, going where the current took me, and it was taking me to New York to say goodbye to that precious baby girl. I had to go home and pack, and tell my babies that their "Cousin Kelly" had died. When I did, Jamie took my face in her hands, looked me straight in the eye and said, "It's okay, Mommy! You'll die, too, someday, and then you'll see her again!" Faith like little children, that's what God says we need. Oh, if I only could.

My Aunt Patty and Uncle Mike came with us to New York. My aunt ministered to me the whole time. She handed me her bookmark on the plane and it read, "Be still and know that I am God" (Psalm 46:10). I was afraid to see my brother who, along with his wife, had been interrogated for hours. I was also afraid to see Alan, who was being investigated for her death because he was allegedly the only one home when the "accident" occurred. Aunt Patty told me that if I felt uncomfortable or attacked, all I had to say was, "Get thee from me, Satan! I rebuke thee in Jesus' name!" And the enemy must flee at the sound of His name! So this was what I did, over and over while I was there.

It was actually good to see my brother. I hugged him, comforted him, listened to him, and even laughed with him as we remembered some of the better times from our childhood. I talked with his wife, Tabitha, and Alan, too. I believed they were both grieving, but I did not believe much of what they said. It seemed to me that they were all plotting, trying to come up with a story. My brother was definitely no stranger to fanaticizing and making up wild stories. I was certain that Alan and Tabitha had learned this too.

It was September 3rd, my daughter Lilly's 4th birthday. I missed it because I was burying my niece. The car pulled up in front of the funeral home. Tabitha's family was already there. When the doors opened, I couldn't move. I didn't want to get out. Peter took my arm and led me in ahead of everyone else. I wouldn't have had the strength to do it on my own.

It was beautiful inside, all purple and frilly with dozens of precious pictures of Kelly everywhere. And so many flowers! Then I saw her in the casket at the front of the room, and I couldn't breathe. My legs stopped working. I couldn't come any closer to her—just lying there so still—because then it would all be real.

The funeral director came up beside me and whispered, "This is the worst part." Then he helped me the rest of the way. I had not realized until I reached the casket that my eyes were closed. When I opened them, I looked down. Kelly looked so peaceful as if she was only sleeping. I wanted to hold her hand, but I didn't want it to be cold for that would mean she truly wasn't coming back.

My hand was hovering just above hers. Then my uncle Mike came over and stood next to me. He said softly, "Okay, Val, we're gonna do this together," and he reached out and put Kelly's small hand into mine. It was cold and stiff just as I feared. Tears gushed down my face, but I didn't want to let go.

"Jesus Loves Me" and "Amazing Grace" played softly over the loud speakers and I soaked in every word. The service was so beautiful and so perfect. There wasn't a dry eye anywhere. My dad looked at me and squeezed my hand. Then he said through tears of his own, "Now she sees!"

We left New York the next day. It was hard for my brother to say goodbye to us. I could tell he hadn't slept much. He couldn't keep anything down and there was fear in his eyes. I think he knew something was terribly wrong and that he would somehow be blamed for his daughter's death. And rightly so! He was her father. He should have been better at it.

Once we got back home, I was on the computer constantly. As the details emerged, I felt more and more anger and guilt. A rope, a sword, computers, clothing and bed sheets were among the pieces of evidence. The authorities found close to 120 cats in Peter's home—70 in the master bedroom alone! There were piles of feces in every room and 20 frozen kittens in the freezer. There were also several dogs, a parrot, an iguana and farm animals, all neglected and all living in the house. Peter claimed it was a working farm, but they never sold anything.

Kelly stank so badly from cat urine that the kids used to throw soap at her on the bus. She never once said anything to us. The nurse brought clothes for her to change into at school, but Peter told her to keep them, so the nurse had her change back before she went home.

Kelly was also asked to leave her backpack outside the classroom because it smelled so bad. My heart sank even more when I learned that this child had been living on only one meal a day. No wonder she had been seen taking food from the garbage cans at school. Her "parents" were starving her.

As I read further, the article said that Peter had been offered services over and over, but he refused. CPS had been called numerous times and had visited three times, and each time they left my niece in that squalor. The lies Peter and Tabitha were telling the police and the media made me sick. The last time I talked to my brother, he heard my kids playing in the background and said, "You take care of them." I hung up without commenting, but rage was boiling inside of me. How dare he tell me to take care of my kids! I know how to take care of my kids. He treated his kid worse than I would treat a dog! I never answered his calls again.

However, that year I realized that I was not taking care of my kids. Tino was. I was obsessed with the investigation and the trial. Tino had been laid off again. He was sick of it. He wanted to go to school like we had talked about. I got a job as an apprentice jeweler. It was what I needed to take my mind off the guilt and pain. But as soon as I got home from work, I was back on the computer or sleeping from depression. I was at odds with my parents because they were denying any wrongdoing by my brother, denying the whispers and concern. I couldn't believe they were so blind, lying and taking the wrong side, and they were angry with me for talking to a reporter and the authorities.

In September 2009, Peter and his wife were convicted of child neglect and endangerment. They were each to serve two years in county jail. A short time later, Alan was convicted of the rape and murder of our little girl, and was sentenced to 25 years to life. Kelly was killed by the one person in that house she believed was her friend. I was beyond remorse. My guilt was smothering me.

A year passed and I was still a wreck. I was willing to try anything to feel normal again. A friend at work told me about her church and it sounded like a good place to start. My marriage was still in shambles and I was desperate. I wouldn't do any more around the house when I stayed home than I thought Tino would do when he stayed home. I had a hard time with intimacy. I didn't feel loved the way I deserved, so I thought, why should I give him anything he wanted?

After what I had been through in my life, I thought all men were the same. I had zero respect for them and their desires, and as hard as I tried, I couldn't stop my mind from putting me in the place of an 11-year-old girl. Tino was on overload with going to work and school (which he had started recently) and then having to come home and deal with me. He held up for as long as he could, but tensions kept building.

I was getting ready for work one day and noticed Tino struggling with the girls. It was his turn. He was trying to get them up and out the door for school. But I ignored him. When he asked if I would help, I said sarcastically, "You never help me in the morning when I'm home and you're getting ready for work." I knew immediately it was the wrong thing to say. I had pushed the wrong button and he snapped.

Tino grabbed the belt from his closet and stormed toward the girls' room. I was screaming. They were screaming. I went after him and told him if he was going to beat anyone, he could beat me. He pushed me against the wall and I came back at him. This, of course, made him even angrier. He shoved me down on the floor, heels over my head. I yelled out, "I want a divorce", while all the kids were crying hysterically.

The next day Tino took the kids to my parents so we could talk. When he got back, we talked some and yelled a lot, and then I left. I told him I wouldn't stay in our home again until he found someone we could talk to—together. I was surprised when he chose one of the pastors at my friend's church. Though we had only met with him once before he moved away, it was the beginning of a true love story. It was also the start of our family going to church regularly.

I also began attending a recovery group, which I desperately needed. My life was about to change, but in a very good way. In Luke 14:26, Jesus says, "If anyone comes to me and does not hate his own father and mother and wife and children and brothers and sisters, yes, and even his own life, he cannot be my disciple." Well, I was right there!

That first night I shared with my group the story about Kelly and all my guilt and anger that had built up over the years. Afterward, the leaders prayed with me. I would come home every Wednesday night a blubbering mess, and Tino was like, "Are you sure this is helping you?" It was. At that point, there was nothing I needed more than a safe place where it was okay not to be okay.

I finally realized that I had worth in God's eyes. God loved me for me. Not for what I could do for Him. He would never turn away from me for anything I did or didn't do. I was created to be in a relationship with Him, but I was fallen. I was a sinner—like everyone else. The Bible told me God's truth in John 3:16, "that

God so loved the world (and me) that He gave His Son's life for me!" He told me that Satan and his demons are constantly trying to make everyone in this world believe his lies; that demonic influence can hang on in families from generation to generation; and if we never learn the truth that Jesus has dominion over them, we will go on believing those lies.

After several weeks in counseling, I learned that my brother Peter was demonic. Even though it was obvious, I was still shocked by this realization. I believed lies upon lies about how life works, about what I "deserved" out of it, and what my role was in it. This I know is true; that if you believe in the Bible, and you believe in Jesus, you must believe in demons too, and be aware of the lies they spread for the father of all lies—the devil himself. One of Satan's greatest accomplishments and grandest of all lies has been convincing this world that he does not exist. But he is every bit as real as God.

Over the next several months, I learned if I truly believed that Christ had died for me and that He paid the penalty for my sins, then I wouldn't go running back to try to pick them up again. I did that with the guilt I carried with me for not trying to help save my precious Kelly because I didn't think I deserved to let the guilt go. Satan didn't want me to let it go. I thought it was my cross to bear, and that putting it down would somehow be letting her down. But who am I to question God?

Jesus went to the cross willingly because He loves me. And He loves you, too. He says in Matthew 11:28-30, "Come to me, all you who are weary and burdened, and I will give you rest. Take my yoke upon you and learn from me, for I am gentle and humble in heart, and you will find rest for your souls. For my yoke is easy and my burden is light." Knowing this has helped me greatly.

It was the same thing with my grief. I knew I needed to heal for my family, for Tino, but I almost didn't want to. I thought that healing would mean letting her go. Someone told me once that "this kind of hurt is like an amputation. You heal, but you're never the same." I know it will be hard, but the Lord says, "Blessed are those who mourn, for they will be comforted" (Matthew 5:4). And I am.

But my anger was crushing me—eating me alive. As hard as I tried, I could not forgive my brother. I thought if I did that, I would be saying it was okay how he treated his daughter—locking her up in squalor, starving her, crushing her spirit, and taking away any hope she might have had. But I was wrong. To forgive simply means that you agree to live with the hurt someone else has caused you, and that you will no longer hold it over their heads. Still, it was difficult.

When a child is made to live in those conditions, being raped and tormented and then strangled, how can anyone forgive this? You can't. But God can. If you're struggling to forgive someone for the pain that they have caused you, ask the Lord to put forgiveness in your heart. You cannot do it alone. Believe me, I have tried. It is impossible. But with God, anything is possible—even this.

Along the way, I realized that I was no more worthy of forgiveness than my brother and his wife, or even Alan for that matter, and as hard as it was to accept, I knew that Christ had died for them too! Being angry didn't make anything better. Anger is poison and it was slowly killing me. I was its prisoner and I wanted out. The Bible showed me the way. It was the Apostle Peter who came to Jesus in Matthew 18:21-22, and asked, "Lord, how many times shall I forgive my brother or sister who sins against me? Up to seven times?" Jesus answered, "I tell you, not seven times, but seventy-seven times." In Mark 11:25, Jesus says, "And when you stand praying, if you hold anything against anyone, forgive them, so that your Father in heaven may forgive you your sins."

At that moment, I imagined myself going to the cross and laying it all down, and then walking away, never to pick it up again. I let Christ take it down to the grave and conquer it. That's when I became a new creation in Him! I was free of demons, aware of their presence and lies; I was free of the crushing guilt, hurt and anger over Kelly's death; I forgave my brother through an act of will, not a feeling. Now I needed to focus on my everyday life that had been a train wreck.

I started hearing words like victim, expectations, and entitlement. I began looking back at my past and at my present everyday behavior toward the people in my life. From my childhood abuse, the abortion, the "sexual slavery" with Brock, my selfishness, the dissatisfaction with my marriage, and my historic inability to say no or face conflict, I started to see how self-focused I had been.

Because I had focused on everything Tino wasn't doing for me, I had failed to see what he was doing for me! I never realized how gravely I was sinning against him every single day. I disrespected him, denied him, and failed to encourage him. I realized that we couldn't communicate because everything he said to me, I took as a personal attack. A pastor I heard once likened chronic fighting to an engine with two pistons. In order for one to keep firing, the other had to fire, but if one stopped, the other would too. It was genius! So I decided to pray for the self-control not to fire back. In Proverbs 12:16, it says, "The vexation of a fool is known at once, but the prudent ignores an insult." I was the quarrelsome wife that "is like a constant dripping of a leaky roof" in Proverbs 19:12.

I prayed for the Lord to fill my heart with a desire for my husband, for the strength to serve him instead of complaining about how he wasn't serving me. I looked for what he was doing right, and there was so much I had missed or misunderstood. I stopped speaking badly about him to everyone. I realized that my husband is God's child too— broken, struggling with sin, in need of grace, love, respect and a Savior. The Lord was faithful and He transformed my heart.

You cannot imagine how different our marriage is now. We are growing, building each other up and able to speak to each other about parenting, about finances, our plans, our dreams, and God. Tino is growing into the spiritual leader of our family, and I'm so humbled by the transformation.

There is so much I am blessed with, but I was seeing everything as a burden. I was like that woman who said she was always angry when she came home because no one else cleaned. Then she realized that she should be happy because the mess meant she had a family. The dirty dishes meant they were fed. This was a breakthrough for me. Proverbs 14:1 says, "The wise woman builds her house, but with her own hands the foolish one tears hers down." I was the wife tearing her house down. I can't tell you how many times I had prayed, "Please, God, when I get home let the house be clean, and the homework be done!" Then when it wasn't (which was pretty much every day), I would flip out.

I learned that God did not make us to be comfortable. He is refining us with fire—and fire often hurts, but it's necessary for growth and for trusting Him more. Eventually I let go of those expectations and began to pray in accordance with His will. "Lord, prepare my heart for whatever I meet when I get home. Provide me the strength, patience and wisdom to accomplish whatever my family needs from me; be it homework, discipline, cooking, cleaning or love." I flip out far less now.

I am not perfect. I continue to struggle, and I still fall short in everything. I am by no means sinless. I just sin less—because I want to. I have hope. I see the transformation, the sanctification He promised. I am a work in progress. His work! My God loves me. He gave His Son for me. When Jesus was crucified, He took all my sins. They were so crushingly heavy for me to bear alone, so He took them from me and dealt with them in the grave.

Never have I known gratitude like this before. My issues with sin don't define me anymore. The devil can no longer use them against me. God had turned everything in my life that was meant for evil into good, for His purpose—even the brutal death of a beloved child.

As it turned out, this tragedy was the worst and best thing that ever happened to me. It was her death that brought me crushingly to my knees, to the foot of the cross, and emptied me of myself. It brought me to my Savior, my God. I am a Christ follower, and nothing and no one can ever separate me from Him now. I am eternally grateful!

The Woman at the Well

To say I lived as far away from a Godly life as anyone ever had would be an understatement. My childhood years were precious and the memories I have inside will never be anything but wonderful. I was protected, loved and deeply cherished by my mother, and adored and spoiled by my father. But when I was thirteen, everything changed—my parents announced that they were getting divorced. I never saw it coming. There were no outward signs of any kind. They never fought in front of me us and they always seemed happy, content, and in love.

I was the middle child of three and was always the one who needed more attention—and would do almost anything to get it. It wasn't that I was a bad child. I just chose to do bad things. I didn't think my parents' divorce was that devastating for me, or at least it didn't feel like it was at the time. But in retrospect, it probably played a huge role in who and what I turned out to be in my early adult life.

After my father moved out, I began to rebel. I cut school in junior high at least once a week. Then I started sneaking out at night with my girlfriend. I tried smoking cigarettes although, thank God, I never took up the habit. I got caught stealing some records and cosmetics from a drug store and was grounded for several months. However, because my dad no longer lived with us and my mother worked all day, I never really felt the total effects of their punishment. I left whenever I wanted. No one ever checked on me so it really didn't matter if I stayed home or not. My grades were average but, then again, no one asked to see them. If it didn't matter to them, it didn't really matter to me either.

When I was fifteen, I moved in with my dad and his new wife. At seventeen, I ended up pregnant by my high school sweetheart—my first love, my first sexual encounter. I had boyfriends before, but I never gave myself to them. Besides, I remembered my mom telling me how wrong it was, so I knew better than to even try. At least it stopped me for awhile, before I just said, "Why not? All my girlfriends are doing it. So I may as well do it, too!"

My boyfriend and I had been together almost four months before we gave into our temptations—now I was with child! I couldn't believe it. In fact, I stayed in denial for several months. But after going through numerous bouts of morning sickness, I finally got up enough nerve to tell my stepmother. I was much too afraid to tell my dad, so I let her tell him—and he was furious! The next day, he told me his plan. "We're going to see Dr. Davis tomorrow. If it isn't too late, he said he'll take care of everything." I had no idea what this meant, but I found out soon enough.

The next morning after I was examined, the doctor announced that the plans had changed. "I cannot terminate the pregnancy because she's almost five months along and it wouldn't be safe for either of them," he explained.

I knew I had caused my dad a great deal of embarrassment and grief and he was desperate to come up with a solution. His next plan was to send me away. "There's a home I read about for unwed mothers somewhere in Montana or Wyoming, and I think it's probably best that you go there and have your baby. They will put it up for adoption and then you can come home and finish high school like nothing happened," he said, feeling relieved that he had finally fixed the problem. But my response put my parents back to square one.

"Daddy, I'll be eighteen before this baby is born! I won't stay in that home or give my baby up! I'll run away and there won't be anything you can do!" I announced defiantly. But before my dad could react, my stepmother interrupted.

"Okay, how about this. How about your dad and I adopt your baby and raise it as our own?" My stepmom had two children from a previous marriage and she and my dad just had a little boy together. I guess they figured one more "kid" wouldn't be that much of a burden. I, however, was appalled!

"No way! I will not be my child's sister!" I screamed. "And you will not be its parents!"

In the meantime, my boyfriend kept pleading for us to get

married. His parents wanted us to, as well. They thought it would be best for everyone under the circumstances. After all, I was having his baby and, once we got used to the idea, we both wanted to keep it.

So at seventeen, just babies ourselves, we began to make our wedding plans. We both needed a note from our parents for permission to get a marriage license. Then three weeks later, we were married by the Justice of the Peace in my father's living room, with a few close friends and family members in attendance. Thankfully, I was able to finish high school with a home tutor who came to our apartment three times a week for the next three months. I never walked down the aisle to get my diploma, but I did graduate.

Over the next five years, my husband and I had two more children. He was an excellent provider and a good person, too—but we were just so young. We didn't know the first thing about the commitment of marriage and, as for me, it was never important enough to even try. I learned that from my parents. My dad was married five times and my mother was married a total of eight. Commitment was not in their vocabulary.

When my young husband and I went through some challenging times, we had no idea how to remedy the situation. No one was surprised when, a short time later, we announced that we were getting a divorce. I was twenty-two, with three young children in tow. It wasn't easy, but I managed—but only by the grace of God. However, at this time in my life, I would have never given God the credit. I didn't even know Him and yet, I knew He was watching over me (even back then) because He had a plan for me and nothing interfered with God's plans (something I learned much later as well).

After the divorce was final, I had a couple boyfriends that I dated before "husband number two" entered my life. By this time, I was desperate. My dad had just divorced my stepmother and I had inherited my little stepsister, a stepbrother (who had Down's Syndromes), and a half brother. I wasn't given any extra compensation for taking my siblings in, but I knew I couldn't just leave them at home alone either. Their mother (my ex-stepmother) was running wild and only went home occasionally to change her clothes. They had no supervision whatsoever.

One night while she was out gallivanting around town, my brothers had left a candle burning in their bedroom on the floor between their beds. During the night, one of their sheets caught fire and destroyed that part of the house. Thankfully, the kids escaped before the fire became too intense. My little sister, who was only eleven at the time, had been left in charge. She could barely take care of herself—let alone two younger brothers. So I brought them all home with me, took them to school every day, fed them, and put a roof over their heads. Husband number two was willing to take us all!

Four months after our wedding, I found out I was pregnant again. Talk about a full house! Ours was overflowing! This man was a decent family man and worked very hard in order for us to have a beautiful home, as well as all the other things we needed and wanted. But what I didn't know was that he was heavily involved with some major drug dealings—selling as well as partaking. A few years later, he was murdered with a single gunshot to his stomach.

My life began to spiral out of control. I was knee-deep in kids and working at a minimum-wage job that barely paid the bills. Soon thereafter, my two older children went to live with their father, who was better able to provide for them. My half brother moved in with my dad when he remarried. My other brother was put in a special home and my little sister stayed with me.

"Husband number three" came and went before I knew what was happening, although he did not go without leaving his mark on my life. Twice I became pregnant and twice I had an abortion. No one ever told me it was wrong. To this day my heart aches for these children that I chose to just throw away, and I still haven't been able to completely forgive myself for this total act of selfishness.

A short time later, I started a new job as a cocktail waitress in a very high class resort and casino and it paid very well. The lifestyle was fast and I was drawn into it quite easily. Soon I was introduced into a world of "high rollers". Most of them were older, distinguished men who had more money than I had ever seen before—or since. As a cocktail waitress, I learned very quickly how to treat these men who could literally change all our lives with one throw of the dice or with a lucky hand of cards, especially when they had too much to drink—and we always made sure they did! The amount of money they would throw at us when they were winning was truly exhilarating.

I was so impressed with their wealth and power and extremely eager to be a part of their world—even if it was only for a night. I dated a couple of them, but I was so young and so very naïve. I look back on some of the choices I made and I can't imagine what I was thinking.

I once dated a guy in the Mafia who had more money than brains. He drove a brand new Rolls Royce and carried a gun everywhere we went. This man also employed a fulltime bodyguard who never left his side. I also had two affairs with married men that lasted longer than any of my marriages thus far. The remorse, shame and guilt from these affairs have yet to go away.

The next few years were a whirlwind of nonstop parties and selfish pleasures. But after a while it became routine and boring. Then I met "husband number four." I had had my fill of the craziness and wanted to be a wife and settle down again.

He, too, was a good man who provided well for my children and me. By this time, there were only two kids living at home. Then three years after our wedding anniversary, my husband and I had a baby of our own. So if you're keeping track, I now had five children—with three different fathers.

I didn't realize it at the time, but I had set such an unstable and ungodly example for all my children. They would be darn lucky if they grew up the least bit normal. But at the time, it wasn't really something I thought about. However, my fourth marriage was doomed (as well) because I was still not sure how to totally commit to someone, nor did I have any biblical knowledge that divorce was wrong.

After five years, when troubled waters rose too high, we both walked out—in different directions—and never looked back. My fourth divorce came shortly thereafter. It wasn't something I bragged about or even admitted to anyone very often. But since this is my story, I am being honest and telling you how it was for me before I surrendered myself to God.

I was still working at the resort and, being newly single, fell right back into the lifestyle I had known before. I needed the money to live and to raise the three children who were still with me. I was a complete mess, lost in a world I had no business being in, but not knowing how to get out either. Drugs were all too available and, although I was never an addict, I certainly did my share.

When I think of the trouble I could have put myself in with the chances I took, I just can't believe that person was me! Therein lies God's plan. I know, without a doubt, that He was watching over me and protecting me each and every time I did something stupid. He intended to use me someday to bring Him glory, and for me to give my testimony as I am doing at this moment. He didn't need me behind bars, or in the gutter, or the graveyard—so He kept me safe. But soon, even God had had enough!

Enter "husband number five"—and oh, the price I paid for this one! He took it all—everything I had; money, dignity, self-esteem, trust, and even part of my spirit. He dragged me through the dirt and back again. He cursed me, beat me, cheated on me, and raped me. He used me. Then he threw me away. It was during this time, when I had nothing left, that I realized just how pitiful and disgusting my life had become; how dirty I felt and how I needed something more.

I was so lost and confused, as well as overwhelmed with grief and guilt—especially when thinking about the impact my life had on my poor children. They were the ones who had to endure the painful impact of all my bad choices and failures—and had not asked for any of it.

Six years later, when husband number five was finally out of my life, I was scared, scarred and nearly broken beyond repair and ready to give up on everything and everyone, which was exactly where God needed me to be—at rock bottom—with nowhere to go but up.

Soon I felt a powerful tugging on my heart. I didn't know exactly what it was, but I heard this Voice inside telling me that I needed to go to church! I had no idea which church, but I knew I had to find one. So one Saturday night, when the kids were with their dads and I was all alone, I got in my car and drove several miles until I ended up in the parking lot of a church. I had attended this church one other time—many years ago—at Easter. I don't even know why I chose this particular church—but God knew. There was something I needed to hear.

The pastor was giving a message on the Samaritan woman at the well in the Gospel of John, in Chapter 4 of the Bible. After Jesus spoke to this woman and told her to drink from His living water so she would never thirst again, the woman said to Him,

"Sir, give me this water that I may never thirst, nor come here to draw." Jesus said to her, "Go call your husband, and come here." The woman answered and said, "I have no husband." Jesus said to her, "You have well said, 'I have no husband,' for you have had five husbands, and the one whom you now have is not your husband; in that you spoke truly."

What! This woman had five husbands? How could this be? Had it not been for the time lapse of 2000 years before, this could have been me sitting there with Jesus! I started to squirm in my seat. My heart slammed against my chest and my eyes flooded with tears. The people around me must have thought I was crazy. They kept looking at me—but I didn't care. I could feel the presence of Jesus. And He was talking to ME!

After Jesus and the Samaritan woman conversed a while longer, she said to Him, "I know that Messiah is coming (who is called Christ). When He comes, He will tell us all things." Jesus said to her, "I who speak to you am He."

This was truly unbelievable! The woman talking to Jesus was a sinner, the worst of the worst—doing everything wrong. And yet, she was smart enough to know that when the Messiah was coming, He will "tell us all things!" As I sat there in my seat, I realized it was time that I knew her Jesus, too.

Before I left church that night, the pastor did an altar call. He asked his congregation, "If there is anyone here tonight who wants to know Jesus personally, and give their life to Him, please come forward."

I slowly got out of my seat and walked to the front of the church along with a few other people. On bended knees, I prayed,

"Father God, Help me! I have done so many things in my life that I regret. I cannot take any of them back. If I could I would. But I can't. I need You to help me, Father. I know I don't deserve it, but I'm asking for Your forgiveness. I want to start over. I know this life I have chosen is not what You want for me. I know, too, that You have been waiting for me to surrender myself to You. And this day, I do. I surrender with all my heart. Please take this messed up heart of mine and give me a brand new one. Let me be 'born again' in You."

I don't know how to explain what happened next. Only someone who has been through it before would know what I am talking about. The heaviness of guilt that I had felt for so long was lifted. My heart felt "new"—as if I had truly been reborn. The feeling that came over me was comforting and warm. I knew in my heart it was God! It had to be! I had never felt anything like it before! It was love; pure, complete, and unconditional love.

This was the turning point in my life. I knew with all my heart that it was God who had led me to that church knowing full well what the pastor was going to talk about—and that I needed to hear it. God opened my eyes and my heart and I fell to my knees in sorrow, remorse, and overwhelming brokenness.

I asked Jesus into my heart that night, and He took my hand—without question and without judgment. He was waiting. And, as I got closer to Him, I learned He had been waiting a very long time.

I was in my forties by this time and had wasted so much of my life. But I knew, too, that there was still so much more life to look forward to. God was growing inside of me daily. Yet, I was by no means perfect. Even after I surrendered myself to Him, I didn't always do the right thing—but I always tried. When I fell, I just got back up and started over. I asked God's forgiveness and He always gave it to me.

We are not strong enough to go through this life alone. Life can be good, but it can also be very difficult at times. However, with Jesus living inside of us, we know we always have a Savior in our corner—One who will fight for us and never leave us no matter what.

I did get married again and, although we both had major issues to work on (separately as well as together), I knew that this time it was for keeps. This time around was definitely "for better or for worse"—and some days they are worse! My husband and I have been tested many times, with trials and challenges that I would have never been able to get through before (nor would I have wanted to). But this time I had a Savior and He had a plan!

It's been more than 20 years and my husband and I are still going strong. This being said, there are still those days when I want to ring his neck and I'm pretty sure that he would like to do the same to me. But we stand firm in our commitment to one another. Satan would be thrilled if we got divorced, but I can tell you with all certainty that that will never happen!

My husband is a good man and a God-fearing Christian and I am so grateful to God for giving me this last chance at love. We both grow closer to Him every day even with every "trial and tribulation" we go through. But divorce is not an option! To take the words of an incredibly Godly woman, Ruth Graham (Billy Graham's wife of more than sixty years), when she was asked if she ever thought of divorcing Billy because he was gone so much, her answer was, "Divorce? Never! Murder? Possibly."

Finally, I understand the true meaning of commitment. It doesn't matter what you go through with your spouse. You always need to work it out, no matter how bad or hurtful it may seem at the time. And forgiving each other is a must! It's all about choices. Love and marriage is a choice—one you have to make every day. And I choose to stay and fight for mine with all my heart. I only wish I had learned this earlier, but I thank God I finally did!

Surprisingly enough, I don't blame my parents for my mistakes. I know they didn't teach me very well on the commitment of marriage, but I knew better than to just throw all those relationships away. Now I walk in living proof that commitment is the key! But (at least for me), it absolutely has to start with God!

I am more blessed than I deserve and there are times when I just don't understand why. Our Father has given me so many beautiful, healthy children and grandchildren—and even great-grandchildren! But I constantly ask, "Why me, Lord? I am so not worthy. I did horrible things for so long, yet You still continue to bless me!" There were children I chose to deny and abort, throwing them away just because they were not wanted or the timing was wrong. Yet, God has been faithful, giving me more children than I ever dreamed I would have.

I am surrounded by love and babies and more humble than I can say. I know I don't deserve it, but evidently God thinks I do.

In spite of everything, God loves me (as He does all His children) and He wants to enrich my life with His blessings—and all these babies are blessings, indeed!

As for my children, they actually turned out far better than they should have, especially with what I put them through. I can tell by the way they live their lives as adults today that my unfavorable influence on them is somewhat obvious, but they are still great kids. Some even have a strong relationship with God—not because of me, but because they discovered Him on their own. I pray constantly that the rest will follow and give their precious lives to Jesus. Then they can teach their own children about Him and how loving and forgiving He truly is. "I surrender them all to you, Lord. Do with them as You will, whatever it takes!"

I live with so much shame and regret and that is something that will never fully go away. I could have been such a good example for my children, not only as their mother, but also as a spiritual leader—but I wasn't. I know the Lord has forgiven me and I hope that, over time, they can learn to forgive me as well. If I could I would go back and do it all again—the right way. But I can't, and I am sorrier than words could ever say.

I try now to be a better grandmother (Nona) than I was a mother, with hope and determination that I can leave a legacy of some goodness inside these little hearts that have so graciously been entrusted to me. I am also going to make sure they all know about the Savior who died for them on the cross and who loves them very much.

And as for those little ones that I just threw away, I know I will see you again one day. And when I do, I will hold you close and kiss you and tell you how much I love you, and that I'm so very sorry I sent you "home" before you had any chance at life down here. But I know in my heart that you have already forgiven me, because you've been with Jesus all this time—and, my children, He has taught you well.

Even though I know I am only a challenge or trial away from the next disaster, I know I can get through anything with Jesus in my heart—guiding my every step. And He does—everyday.

I realize that I am not yet what I should be or what I could be. But I thank God I'm not what I used to be either. I can never thank Him enough for all He has done for me in my life and how He has given me a hope I never knew before. Praise and glory to Him forever!

"Hell is the highest reward that the devil can offer you for being a servant of His" ~ Billy Sunday

Thy Kingdom Come
His Will Be Done

My name is Katie. I am 27 years old as I sit and write this story. It's been almost 10 years since the most frightening and destructive thing happened to me, which changed my life forever and rocked me to my very core.

When I was little, my relationship with my father was rocky from the very start. In fact, when I think back, I barely have any good memories of him at all. I don't have one single memory of him ever being kind to me. The memories I do have are of him constantly screaming at me, and then me crying hysterically as I would curl up into a ball of sadness and pain. Then moments later, my father would be going about his normal routine, carrying on like nothing ever happened. Did he not just hear what he said to me? Evidently not, for each time it happened, he made me feel as if I was the one who was crazy. In every instance, I was constantly being blamed, manipulated and controlled.

By the tender age of seven, I had pretty much given up on him. I was so tired and tortured by all the unfulfilled promises, and of being verbally and emotionally crippled with no apologies or closure. Time after time his manipulation and mind games left me feeling like there was something wrong with me. So, at seven years old, I shut down. I was done with him.

Life started to have no meaning for me. It moved so slowly and deliberately. Every day was filled with anxiety and fear, and always in the direction of perpetual nothingness. How long must I suffer? When would the torment end?

When I was 14, things started to get even more intense on a whole new level. I was no longer enduring just the verbal and emotional abuse. Things had moved to the extremely psychological and somewhat physical level as well, pushing me further into darkness and depression. And although I wasn't brutally beaten or anything, my father always had a way of making me feel as if the beatings could happen—if he wanted them to. He did this on purpose, to show his power.

My father spent all four of his college years as a wrestler. Because of this, he had a special knack for using his body in such a way that made you feel trapped and cornered. It gave him great pleasure to try to take away your sense of peace and personal space. This became a game that he challenged himself to daily, which completely stripped away my sense of personal safety. Hence, I made the decision to start sleeping with a huge knife under my pillow.

From the outside we looked like a perfectly normal family. Through other people's eyes, my father appeared to be a great dad, attending every recital, play, music concert, as well as volunteering for every field trip and every class-parent opportunity that was available. It was everything a normal, good parent would do. Except that for him, the reason he did it wasn't out of love or compassion; it was out of necessity to be in control. He had to control everything. He needed it. He craved it. He would do anything to obtain it—and he did. Not only was he on top of everything I did at school, it was by far 100 times worse at home.

Every time I invited my girlfriends over for a sleepover, my dad had to make sure he was the central part of it, but not in the fun "cool dad" way. It was more in an "awkward and overbearing" way, like staying in the room with us—uninvited. My friends would look at me and I knew what they were thinking; "Is he ever going to leave?" Sometimes we'd all stop talking, hoping he'd get the hint. But our silence didn't bother him one bit. He always stayed, always intruded, and always had to have control of every situation—sometimes without ever saying a word.

His obsession to control me went even further when I later suspected that he had been sneaking into my room when I wasn't there, to go through my belongings and to read my diary. I could tell he had been there because he never put my things back the way I had them. One day he went through my collection of DVDs and broke all the ones he didn't think I should have. Then he put all the broken pieces back in their container, but he never said a word. He just did it. Oh, the joy of going to watch your favorite movie and finding nothing but these shattered bits of DVDs instead. When I saw him the next morning, his face gave nothing away that he had done anything, and the issue was never addressed. Once again, I was left to feel like I had imagined the whole thing. It was torment…pure and simple. And my father enjoyed every moment. My rage exploded.

When I was 15, right before my parents divorced, I remember three things that stayed with me for a very long time: My father throwing my mom against the wall; me screaming at him and cursing like a sailor; and me realizing that I could have killed him without an ounce of remorse—literally, killed him. What an absolutely horrifying realization that was. But it was real. I was completely prepared to defend myself and my mom.

It's terrifying to look back and remember the blind seething hatred that overwhelmed my body, feeling as if my blood were boiling through my veins, and seeping down into my soul. The realization that I could despise someone so much and that I could have actually killed him without even batting an eye was horrifying enough. Then to think about this person being my father, the one who was supposed to be protecting and nurturing me, went way beyond any logic I could fathom. Nonetheless, I knew it was only a matter of time before I would have ended his life, or he would have ended mine.

I share these grim details of the experiences I had with my father and how it was back then for a reason. Now I will share what happened next on my road trip to hell—and then the glorious meeting with my "true" Father. Before I do, there's one very important detail I left out of this story. My dad is a pastor. Yes, a man of the Church. Not only was he a pastor, he was a very well respected pastor, theologian, and even a teacher at one of the top, more prestigious colleges in the country. This fact is what confused me the most and sculpted my viewpoint on religion and life.

I was still only 15 when I made a very crucial decision that would impact me beyond anything I could ever imagine—the life-shattering decision that there was no God. There couldn't be. I remember determining this as if it were only yesterday. I was standing outside on the sidewalk in front of my house on a sunny, beautiful day. I decided that I needed to seriously figure out if God existed. So I thought about my dad. I pictured him as a man of God, a pastor of a church, dressed in his ornate robe, and praying over people who were crying and accepting Jesus as their Lord and Savior. Then I thought about him coming home and screaming, throwing my mom around, continuously hurting me—basically ruining our family and destroying my sense of safety. With those memories I made the most logical rationalization I could; there is no possible way that there could be a God. And with that, my conscience was free. I skipped down the sidewalk and went on with my day not realizing the weight of that one decision. What I also didn't realize was the fact that demonic beings were lying in wait…ready to devour.

The day after the divorce, I felt as if I was finally free. I no longer had to deal with this horrible man—my "dad"—on a daily basis, and there were no more of his ridiculous rules.

I joined a friend at his house and he had a bunch of other guys over who I had never met before. We all went across the street to one of their houses, and it was there that I got completely wasted—totally and ridiculously drunk for the first time. I actually smoked pot for the first time as well (without even realizing it) and became even more wrecked.

That day is in snippets of clouded memory: Me peeing a million times from drinking too much beer and watching the room spin every time I looked in the bathroom mirror; someone being mad at me for drinking the majority of a 30-pack of beers which they had brought for everyone; a cop who was there smoking pot with us and who had threatened to beat his wife with a fire poker; and me ending up in some guy's bed. But the grand finale was me walking down the middle of the road toward my mom, who was waiting in her car for me with my 5-year-old brother in the backseat. I use the word "walking" here very lightly, as it was more of a drunken, stumbling, "barely able to stand" walking. What a way for a 15-year-old to start breaking in her newly acquired freedom!

It's amazing that even when I was sinning beyond anything I had ever done before, I was somehow protected from getting raped; I didn't get hit by an oncoming car while staggering down the road; and I didn't give my poor mom (who was going through a terrible divorce) a heart attack when I hopped into the car a complete drunken mess, which she noticed immediately. It was not a fun ride home.

This was the day I referred to as the beginning of my descent into hell. From the ages of 15 until almost 17, I pretty much spent my days doing anything and everything, but to the extreme. Unfortunately, it didn't stop there. It got even worse. If I thought the torment from my dad was unbearable, I had no grid to even compare what my battle was about to look like.

I actually started dating the guy whose house I had gone to, the same guy who I had been in bed with earlier when I was drunk and high. He was the one who ran everything. There was quite an eclectic group of people that hung out at his house. Besides the psychotic corrupt cop and my new "for the moment" boyfriend, there were several gang members, some 20-plus-year-old guys sleeping with 12-year-old girls, and a few drug dealers as well. All of this bizarre activity was happening right down the street from my house in a very pleasant, upper-class neighborhood. This house of questionable tenants was conveniently located within a 15-minute walking distance from my house, so that I could enjoy my debauchery daily while my mom thought I was just hanging out with my girlfriends.

I eventually broke up with the one guy, and I started dating one of the other guys who hung out with us. (Not that it mattered. I would hook up with whoever I wanted when we were dating anyway.) But this new guy, well, he was very different. He not only involved himself in drugs, sex and whatever else went on in that house, but he was also satanic. He actually and purposefully worshiped the devil. It was at this time that my life went completely off the charts.

I apologize to those of you who are about to read this who have the meaning of life confined in a neat little box, believing that "you live, you die and that's it". I am about to stretch your theology a bit, and I mean to do so as politely but honestly as possible.

Suddenly a whole new world was thrown in my face—one I had never known—the unseen world of Satan, a world of the occult and grotesque. What got even scarier was when I actually started to see and experience this demonic world. Even though I grew up Christian, and I knew you weren't supposed to "do that kind of stuff", it wasn't enough to stop me from being around it and eventually experimenting with it.

From the very moment I started dating this guy (who I will just refer to as "satanic guy") I gradually began falling further into darkness myself. I now know that we were born into a war and there is a spiritual realm where the enemy of our souls (Satan) is out to kill, steal and destroy us and everything in our lives. I also know that Satan was on a mission to get me into his clutches, but I refuse to give him any of the glory here, so I am not going to dwell on my dark experiences very long. But I have to mention some of this darkness so you will know how very lost I was and the creepy spiritual things I encountered that pulled me further into fear and anxiety.

My life had flipped upside down. I went from not believing in God, to realizing He was real, and then absolutely hating Him with every fiber of my being. I dated satanic guy for a while and we met up with some friends who were into the spirit world. I started dabbling with horoscopes, tarot cards, signs and omens, psychics, astral projection, aura's, hypnotism, and anything else supernatural that I could get my hands on. All the while, I was constantly getting drunk, smoking pot, having sex, chain smoking cigarettes, cursing, lying, and even stealing to a ridiculous extent.

One evening, satanic guy and I were in the basement where my dad's study used to be. It was completely empty except for a small door that opened up to the sump pump. As we were sitting there on the floor in the dark, something on the other side of that door started knocking like it wanted out. How could anyone want to go in there? I thought. Even as a joke. It was dark and dank and no place for anything human. The pounding grew louder and I nearly jumped out of my skin, panic stricken and hysterical. I ran screaming up the stairs while satanic guy tried to pull me back. He begged me not to say anything to my mom, but at this point I knew I could not be consoled, especially by him. I knew what was behind the door wasn't human and it terrified me. I wanted my mom.

Another time I remember sitting in class during my sophomore year trying to take a final exam and barely being able to concentrate. It took everything I had to hold my pencil still. I felt as if something was trying to move my hands or take over my body. I would always see faces whenever I closed my eyes. I even had a friend tell me that she would see grotesque faces in her head whenever she came near me. I constantly felt something watching me from outside my bedroom window. At night there would be tapping and knocking on my walls, and my electronic games, which I kept in the closet and were turned off, would randomly come on. My nightmares were persistent, especially ones about being possessed. I continued to spiral out of control.

After satanic guy broke up with me, I went further into depression and I became a cutter. I used to sit in the shower and cry while I pulled the blades out from my disposable razor (completely destroying my thumbs in the process), then I would use them to cut myself. On occasion, I would also use a lighter to burn my skin. However, the physical pain I would experience was only a temporary distraction to the mental pain I fought through every day. In fact, I would often get high on Ambien and take an over abundance of NyQuil daily just so I didn't have to be awake. To add to this, I was also bulimic. I just could not handle life any longer. I think it's safe to say that this was the worst time of my life.

While all of this was going on, my level of fear and anxiety were at an all-time high. The terror I had gone through with my dad never left, and I had become so aware of the spirit realm it nearly scared me to death. Even though I was pursuing it with full force, I felt as if I had no will power of my own. I was absolutely petrified, but my fear did not stop me from going deeper.

I went to Salem, Massachusetts with a friend and we went on a ghost/witch tour. I thought it would be fascinating. Throughout the tour, I took countless photographs. When I had the film developed, in almost every one of the pictures were orbs of light with horrifying distorted faces. I could barely force myself to look at them, let alone keep them as souvenirs. I couldn't dump them fast enough.

One day I was sitting on the sofa at that same friend's house watching the Exorcist, when suddenly I felt this huge hand swipe against my back and then the light next to me clicked and turned off. It scared me so badly that I ran out of the house and onto her porch, and I refused to come back inside. My friend wasn't even fazed because she was used to the "beings" being in her house. I, on the other hand, was not okay with it.

Many nights I would wake up only to realize I couldn't move. When I looked up I saw this huge black blob floating over me while something of great force held me down in my bed. I tried with all my strength but I couldn't get up or speak. My bed would move all the time. I'd just be sitting on it and it would shake as I felt something like a "swoosh" of electricity go through it. If all of this wasn't eerie enough, there were also nights when I would wake up with my arms completely raised in the air, as if something invisible were holding them up, reaching for something that wasn't there. I later learned my mom was having her arms held up in the middle of the night as well. Whatever demonic beings I had allowed into my house through my sin was now messing with my family as well.

Oh my mom…my poor mom. The things I put her through. That she stills loves me is a miracle in itself. She was a Christian all the way through high school. However, it wasn't until sometime during her marriage to my dad that she really understood what it meant to be a Christian, and fully accepted Jesus into her life.

Sometime before the divorce process my mom had a conversation with God. "Lord, You tell me to pray when I need You. You tell me that prayer is good and that it works for Your will. But, Lord, prayer doesn't seem to be working for me right now. So if what You say is true, that prayers really truly do work, please, Lord, save my marriage." But He didn't. This was when my mom decided that she would never pray again. If God didn't answer, what was the point?

However, all that changed when one day—near the end of my horrific time period of being lost and into total darkness—my mom was holding a laundry basket full of clothes and walked into my room. There, above my bed, she saw this huge, black floating blob. My mom dropped the laundry basket and started screaming at Satan and telling him that he couldn't have me. "Get away from her, Satan. In the name of Jesus, get away. You cannot have my daughter! I claim her for Jesus!"

My mom and I had been very close before my parents divorced. However, she had no clue what had happened to me afterward, but she knew there was something very wrong, and she was very concerned. She thought I had gone crazy or had become schizophrenic. Sadly, I wasn't just acting crazy. I was possessed. Satan and his demons had a hold on me and would not let go. When I finally realized what was happening, I was petrified.

My mom was deathly afraid of me during this time and we grew a part. However, after she literally saw a form of this darkness hovering over my bed, she had no other choice but to pray. God had opened her eyes to see into the spirit realm and showed her that this was a serious demonic attack on our lives. After that she started praying harder and more faithfully. I fully believe what happened next was because of her prayers.

One night I was being tormented so badly and was so scared that I couldn't sleep. I finally got up and went into my mom's bedroom and crawled into bed with her so that I wouldn't be alone. It had been a year and a half of hell and we were both exhausted. This was the night before my last day of my sophomore year—a night I will never forget.

I didn't realize it, but when I had left my room, the demons had followed me into my mom's bedroom. I had left to escape the knocking and clicks that happened on my walls and window but as soon as I got into bed with my mom, the tapping on her closet doors started. Tap, tap, tap. Knock, knock, knock. They wouldn't stop.

After a while my mom said she couldn't take it anymore and got out of bed. With great strength, determination and exhaustion, she stood in the middle of the room and started crying. She called out to Jesus, and she just kept praying and saying, "Jesus, You need to save my daughter, please save my daughter, please save my daughter… " I remember sitting up in bed in the dark watching her pray and I heard a voice inside my head that wasn't my own say, "Aww, how cute, she's praying to her God." The voice was in a very dark and condescending tone.

The next thing I knew I was in my mom's bathroom ten feet away. I can't even tell you how I got there. It is completely missing from my memory. I found myself sitting on the floor crying, leaning over the toilet and shaking uncontrollably. The room was so bright and my body felt really weird. I honestly don't know how to describe what this feeling was like; something along the lines of being electrocuted. I was light headed, and it seemed as if my insides were missing. The entire ordeal of God removing all darkness from me had taken such a toll on my body that I honestly thought I was going to stop breathing and die. Fortunately, I did neither.

It was then that I saw for the first time what true love was all about. God, the God of the universe, who handcrafted me in my mother's womb, who had been with me through all of my sin, my hurt, and my shame; who had loved and protected me when I was in places I should not have been, had come to rescue me. His face shined on me like no other love I had known before. He reached inside of me that night, ripped out all the demons from my body, and then gave me a choice—I could either follow Him, or continue to follow Satan. I chose to follow Him.

My mom and I went into my room and she started telling me about Jesus. We sat there on my bed together for hours, and every time she would say His name "Jesus" my alarm clock would start blaring. It scared me so bad that after the third time we had to unplug it. There was an insane battle in the spirit realm in my room that night. Satan was battling for my soul with everything he had—but so was Jesus, and since Jesus holds all the power and isn't threatened by any amount of darkness, through whatever the enemy was doing that night, Jesus kept me safe and was the victor.

I was terrified by everything going on, but my mom prayed over and over, asking calmly in faith for the Holy Spirit to come. Before the night was over, I had this overwhelming peace wash over me. I don't know how long we talked and prayed after that, but we were both so exhausted that we finally needed to sleep. We went back to my mom's room to go to bed, even though I wasn't sure how much sleep I would be able to get.

I had absolutely no idea what happened that night. My only thought was how will I ever feel safe again when I sleep? But God knew. When I got back into bed, I literally felt this capsule-shaped entity surrounding my body, like a dome. It was so odd yet so comforting. I wasn't sure what it was, but I slept better than I had in years. It wasn't until years later that I learned Christians often pray for "a hedge of protection" around them to keep them safe. I realized that this was what God, in His abundant grace, had done for me that night.

That incredible night completely changed my life. I clearly and undeniably became a brand new person overnight. I immediately had no desire to do the same things I had been doing for so long. I stopped drinking and getting drunk. I stopped smoking pot and cigarettes. I stopped cutting and burning myself. I stopped throwing up after I ate. I stopped stealing and doing all the other crap I was doing. I had been made brand new in Him. The fact that no matter how broken I was and how far away Satan had taken me, that God could reach me and make me into something beautiful, was truly a miracle.

When I stated earlier in my story that I was somehow protected from getting raped, hit by a car, etc., I finally had my answer—it had been the hand of God all along. So let's just pause here to note how completely Sovereign and amazing God is.

To this day, I have never spoken to my father. He still preaches and teaches at the same very prestigious college, one of the top in the country. I would never do anything to hurt him or to bring him shame. I would not want to have the people God allowed him to lead to salvation ever question their faith for the wrong reasons by looking at my father, as I did, if his true actions were brought out into the light. There has been enough hurt and pain already. I have truly forgiven him. But I don't trust him enough to want him in my life. What he did to me is now between him and God. I will let God handle it. "For we know him who said, "It is mine to avenge; I will repay," and again, "The Lord will judge his people" (Hebrews 10:30).

The one thing I was unable to change was my "sexual promiscuity". My shame and immense hurt in that area would not allow me to release this lifestyle. It was the only thing from my past that stayed with me, and it nearly ate me alive. It's not that I didn't want to stop doing the sexual, immoral stuff; I couldn't! That part of me was still broken. I knew I was supposed to give God all of me; all of my life, but that was the one thing I just could not seem to let Him have. It was the only thing I felt was damaged beyond repair and could never be restored. Good news for me, I was wrong.

Several years later, I had the second most important experience in my life. It was when I met the Holy Spirit for the first time. I started watching podcasts online of International House of Prayer (IHOP) in Kansas City. I saw people doing odd things like laughing uncontrollably, shaking and falling on the floor, and speaking different languages. I had no idea what was going on. It was strange but also fascinating. I wanted to know more so I continued to watch.

I learned that this bizarre behavior happened to many people throughout the Bible. It's when the Spirit of God comes upon our bodies and we kind of short circuit—if you will—because God is so intense and awesome that sometimes our bodies can't handle it. In 1Corinthians 12, it talks about the gifts of the Spirit, one of which includes speaking in tongues, which is the different language phenomenon I was watching. I cried out, "God, if this is You, then I want it!"

I buried myself in books about the Holy Spirit and read Bible stories where He showed up and completely rocked the ground His people walked on. I begged God to let me experience Him, and one day He did just that. I finally got spiritually slammed in a church service (with a real pastor who really loved Jesus), and my life, once again, was completely flipped around. However, unlike all the other times where I was dealing with the occult and demonic spirits which brought fear, for the first time I encountered the Living Spirit of God with all of His joy and peace.

I eventually and willingly handed over my sex life to God, and I watched as He gently and firmly pulled the ugly things out of my heart and life. It was heart surgery at its deepest and most effective. Finally, there it was—purity—and it was all mine! My heart was fully and completely restored. The part of me that I kept untouched from my Creator for so long and allowed men to create something evil instead had finally been washed cleaned. Even if I messed up again, I knew God was waiting right there for me, to forgive me and help me get it right the next time. My sin was already paid for by the blood of Jesus.

Our lives and bodies are like a house, with windows and doors. When we do certain things that God says not to do, not because He's trying to be mean or keep us from something we want, but because He's a loving Father and knows what's best for us, we open up those windows and doors to the enemy of our souls—Satan. For me, I had almost every door flung wide open with a giant flashing neon light that said "Welcome". Through having promiscuous sex, doing drugs, cutting myself, practicing the occult, and having a heart filled with anger and fear, I let the demonic spirits into my life at full force. But by the loving kindness of my wonderful Father in Heaven who heard my mom's sobbing cries for the salvation of her daughter, who saw how broken and scared I was, who knew me from before I was born and saw the damage that my earthly father had done—even though I rejected God and cursed Him and never asked for Him—God came and saved me and changed my life forever.

No matter where you are right now, whether you're reading tarot cards, or in bed next to your boyfriend; no matter where you have been, there is nothing that can keep you away from the love of Jesus. There is no sin too big that God cannot wash away. Just come to Him exactly as you are; soiled and broken, and He will wash you clean and restore to you everything that has been lost. ***I have seen the enemy and his power, but I have met THEE God, and I will never be the same.***

This is my self portrait. It is probably the most personal piece of artwork I have ever done. I bought a huge canvas and decided to do this picture, but for months I couldn't figure out exactly how I wanted it to look. I'm an artist, but painting is fairly new to me, especially painting people. I battled for a long time with different concepts and ideas, color schemes, and the ever-nagging thought that I might not even be able to paint a portrait very well.

Then one day I sat down. I began to pray and asked God what He thought I should paint. That's when it hit square in the face! I was slammed with the idea of doing a self portrait of how God sees me—pure and white as the driven snow.

For the majority of my life I didn't know who I was to God. But over the last few years He has revealed to me how precious we all are to Him; how much we are loved and adored, and how, when we sincerely ask Him for forgiveness, He totally wipes the slate clean and sees us as nothing but pure. It took a lot of praying and waiting on God to figure out how to paint me, but I believe I finally reached the vision He had in mind.

Out of all the things God has done for me, purity has been the greatest gift. I decided to paint myself in a white dress, spotless and without blemish. For despite what I have done in my past, in God's eyes, it is all washed away. In the Bible we are promised garments of white (Revelation 3:5), a crown of glory (1 Peter 5:4), and to sit on a throne (Revelation 3:21). So I painted all of those things because they are wonderful promises from God.

The first night after I painted this, I experienced the most vivid, horrific nightmares all night, ones of being raped and other terrible sexual atrocities. Throughout the night I would wake up and cry out, "Oh God. What is happening?" Then I would fall right back into the nightmares. In the wee small hours of the morning, I woke up again and decided to sit up and try to get a grasp on reality. Feeling completely violated by the nightmares, I sat there and prayed a silent prayer, asking God to help me deal with whatever this was. God is good and He opened my heart to answers. I soon realized that I was spiritually under attack.

Without the least thought of fear or consequence, I had taken on this huge task of painting me through God's eyes and hadn't even realized what kind of impact it would have on the spirit realm. Nor did I care. But Satan, being Satan, was trying to make me feel filthy and defiled. He was trying to get me into a state of mind where I wouldn't want to finish my painting because I would feel so useless and degraded. When I realized what was going on, I laughed so hard and prayed out loud against these useless satanic dreams. Afterward, I put my head back on my pillow, closed my eyes, and had a beautiful, peaceful sleep the rest of the night.

The next day the weight of what happened fully hit me. If the enemy was that disturbed and upset at my painting of glorifying God, then how excited and honored must God be for me to do this painting for Him? The fact that I finally know who I am in Him—and I am able to confidently stand and declare it—is such a joy to His heart.

So this painting is for Him. And to everyone else out there like me, who has led a less than perfect life, know that you are loved. There is nothing you could ever do to change the way God feels about you. You are the desire of His heart. You are His magnificent creation who was made in His image. His self portrait shines through all of us.

"So God created mankind in His own image, in the image of God He created them; male and female He created them. God saw all that He had made, and it was very good" (Genesis 1:27, 31).

Broken But Not Destroyed

My mother raised me alone. I never knew my biological father. I was told that he was often in a drug-induced state. My mother left him when he began beating her and punching her in the stomach while she was pregnant with me. I grew up the typical "momma's boy" and the only father figure I had was my grandfather who passed away when I was six, yet I still have fond memories of him taking me fishing regularly. Although we never went to church, my mother taught me right from wrong and instilled in me a sense of morality and good ethics. All things considered, I was normal and healthy.

At nine years old, my life changed drastically when my mother announced to me that I was going to have a new "Daddy." I did not know this man and barely even recall seeing my mother with him prior to this announcement. Shortly after, we moved from our small town of Luling, Texas, to the big city of Austin. My new "Daddy's" name was Leslie and he came with a bonus—his son Linus.

Not long after the marriage, Leslie started to abuse me. First it was mental abuse and then it became physical as well. My new father's favorite thing was to slap me for any reason he deemed necessary. He instilled fear and hatred in me from the very beginning. There was name calling and demeaning insults on a daily basis. He once even tried to kill me by rigging his truck door to fly open to make it look like an accident. As he turned sharply into oncoming traffic, I flew out of the cab and rolled onto the street, but miraculously I survived.

Sad as it was that this man wished me dead, Linus was even worse. We discovered later that he had been certified as "legally insane" by the State of Texas. Linus, at nine years old, was on enough Codeine to knock out an adult, yet he still only slept a few hours a night. I believe he was demon possessed (or at least oppressed). There was a time that he actually set fire to the apartment when my mother was sleeping because, as he put it, "I wanted you to die!" He would often ransack my room, and one time I woke in the middle of the night to find him urinating on me.

After several years of being subjected to physical and mental abuse—in every way imaginable—by both Leslie and Linus, I began to withdraw. My mother loved me but due to her several operations that rendered her disabled, she turned a blind eye (for the most part) out of necessity for survival. I felt, and was, completely alone.

Due to the daily stress and abuse, I began to lose my hair. By the end of the third year, I had a five-inch bald spot (in diameter) on the top of my head. I also developed a serious stuttering problem. All this added to the problem, even when I was at school, because I was now being mistreated and bullied due to my appearance and the stuttering.

I hated Leslie and Linus and despised my mother for allowing all of this to go on. My mother sent me to a psychologist who informed her that I was on the verge of a nervous breakdown and needed to be removed from the situation immediately. I was also sent to a doctor who performed a series of hair growth injections without any success. At one point, feeling more desperate than ever before, I crept into my parent's room with a baseball bat. I raised the bat above my sleeping stepfather's head and stood there for what seemed like hours, so much so that my arms ached from holding it up. I had every intention of killing him. But thankfully, for whatever reason, I relented and left the room. Leslie never knew of the incident. His abuse never stopped.

This lifestyle we endured continued on until my mother started being abused as well. She finally put an end to it by divorcing Leslie. The two of us literally had to hide from him for months. When we returned back to the house, we found a note he had written to my mom. It said, "I love you Pam" in his own blood that covered one whole wall in the living room.

Within a few months, my hair started growing back and I was

beginning to feel better. But now my mother was seeing someone else. In fact, he was helping her with the divorce and shielding her from Leslie. His name was Bob. Bob was a Vietnam veteran and had some serious issues himself. He was not filled with hate and psychotic behavior as Leslie and Linus, but he was pretty messed up. A victim of neglect from his own parents, who had him enlist in the army at the age of seventeen, Bob only knew how to do things by being tough. Seeing me must have been nauseating to him—the epitome of weakness.

Six months later, my mother remarried again and suddenly I had a new stepfather. I wanted to trust and open up to him, but I was too damaged. It was not long after, that Bob began to "work on me". He taught me martial arts and how to be a man from his view point. I was never slapped again, but there was certainly an element of mental abuse as he employed the military technique of "breaking me down to build me up" (like that was something I needed). I was pushed mentally and emotionally to the point where, instead of a breakdown, I just completely shut down. I developed the ability to turn off my emotions at the flip a switch. From that point on, I was somewhat immune to his various techniques of "breaking me". He tried for years—through insults, physical threats, and ingenious methods of punishments, but I endured all of it with a stone face. I was numb. His techniques failed.

We were considerably poor and could not afford to run the air conditioner in the house, and often ran short on groceries as well. At that time, I was about 14 and was doing lawn work for several regular customers. I saved the money I made whenever I could, but it wasn't long before my mother would borrow it for groceries. Not long after that, the "borrowing" was a thing of the past and I was expected to give all of my money to them to purchase food.

I spent the next few years buying our food, cooking it, serving it, and then cleaning up by myself as my parents watched TV. This was "normal" as far as I knew. This was about the same time that I had my fill of being picked on at school. I also forced myself not to stutter. My hair had grown back and I was becoming a young man (at least in the physical sense). I started listening to hard rock music and stood up for myself enough to stop the bullying at school. I never became a bully—I hated them—but was determined not to ever become victimized by them or anyone else again.

Then my world erupted once again. I started to notice my mom and Bob fighting more than normal. I didn't care for either of them, but the possibility of being without a stepfather was rather appealing. When I was 16, they divorced. Bob never even spoke to me—he was just gone. It was during this time that I went to one of my first parties. I was still a virgin and looking to change that as soon as I could.

At the party, I met a 19 year old girl named Brenda, and that night I accomplished my mission. I was "in love." We began seeing each other regularly, and shortly thereafter, I moved into her apartment. My mother had just had another surgery and was unable to care for herself, but that didn't affect her voice at all. Boy, could that woman yell! Every time I stopped by the house to pick up some of my things, that was all she would do. I would casually walk through to my bedroom, gather whatever I needed and walk past her out the door where Brenda was waiting in her car. We could still hear her yelling as we drove away—and I could care less.

Within a few months, Brenda was pregnant. We were informally engaged and decided to get married. I was in high school when we took our vows and still in high school when we had a beautiful son who we named Colton.

Just prior to all this, I had met a man "who God used" to change my life. We both had motorcycles, which was our common bond and brought us together. His name was Baxter and he was a real character. A former drug dealer, Baxter had just given his life to Christ, shaved off his tri-colored Mohawk, and was on fire for the Lord. Along with spending time with me as a friend, he began to share the gospel with me, but I wasn't the least bit interested. All I knew was that my life was as good as it had ever been, and I didn't feel the need for anything else.

I had a basic belief in God (whatever that means) and I considered myself a "good" person. What did I need to be religious for, much less a Jesus freak like Baxter? After a few months of Baxter preaching to me, I had had my fill. I decided that I wasn't going to hang around him anymore. I went over to his house and found him sitting on the couch in the dark. When I asked him what he was doing, he said, "I'm praying for you, Ray. And God has a message He wants me to share with you."

I had no idea what was going to happen next, but I had to know what this message was. So I asked. "What is God telling you to tell me, Baxter?" And Baxter did not mince words when he said, "God told me that you're not turning to Him because everything is going so good for you and that you didn't feel the need for Him. So as a result, He told me to tell you that your life was going to fall completely apart (via God) so that you would seek Him."

Well, that was it! I didn't need to hear anymore. I had had enough and I decided not to see Baxter again. I left his apartment, thinking he was off his rocker and had done a bit too many drugs in his life. But then, almost immediately, everything Baxter said would happen, happened. My life began to unravel. Within weeks, everything that could have gone wrong did—and then some. Brenda and I were fighting so intensely that she called off our engagement in her last trimester. I was losing it and all the time I literally had not given any thought or credit to what Baxter had told me—his "message from God".

The last day of my life (as I knew it), I was riding to work on my motorcycle and suddenly remembered all that Baxter had shared with me. This was when I went into what I call "God shock" (the sudden realization and belief that God is real!) I decided I would become a Christian. But then the thought came to postpone it. I was going to do it, but not now because things weren't that bad yet. This was the moment when the devil tried to take my life.

I literally had two visions in broad daylight. The first vision was when I saw myself in a terrible wreck, which caused me to slow down. The second vision was when I saw myself in a minor wreck where I picked up my bike and dusted myself off. I could literally hear a voice telling me to "Go ahead, have a wreck... it'll be okay." By the time I snapped out of it, I was yards away from the sharp curve in the parking lot of the mall where I worked. I always tried to take this curve faster and faster every day. Well, even though I was still braking from the first vision, I was unable to make the turn in time and had to "lay down" the bike so I wouldn't hit the curve head on.

The accident was bad. I wrapped my bike around a pole and I slid until I hit the curb. I split my helmet, flew up in the air and landed on the edge of the 75 foot cliff. I remember looking at my bike first then cussing loudly. Next, I looked at myself and this was when the pain hit. I was covered in blood and practically naked from sliding so far that my clothes were actually ripped off my body (bikers call it street pizza). Someone must have called 911, as I heard the sirens getting closer. In the ambulance were two male nurses who held me down while they scrubbed the asphalt out of my open wounds. It was the most painful experience I had ever been through. Brenda met me at the hospital and they said I could go home if I took it easy. She drove me to our apartment and helped me get into bed. She also informed me that we would talk when she got back.

As soon as Brenda shut the door I broke—finally. What Baxter was unable to do, God did. I cried like a baby (something I hadn't done in over six years). Contemplating what had just happened, I concluded that the devil tried to take my life via the second vision before I gave it to God, and God spared my life via the first vision that caused me to brake and not go over the cliff. In the shock of it all, I was ready to surrender my life to God, but I didn't know how. I didn't remember anything about Baxter's preachings on becoming a Christian. But then it came... it was like I was hearing a tape recorder replaying everything he had told me…"You must give all to Him, take Him as your Lord (Boss) and Savior. Your life will no longer be your own. Turn away from all your sin, ask His forgiveness and surrender to Him... that is being born again." You could have offered me any amount of money and I could not have recited any of that, but the Spirit made it loud and clear and that was exactly what I did. Desperation? Yes. But sincere nonetheless. I immediately felt cleansed, forgiven, and accepted. I was overjoyed!

I peeled myself off the sheets and went over to Baxter's apartment. There I found him and his Christian roommate waiting for me, as if they knew I would be coming. I told them the news and they literally jumped up and down yelling, "Praise God." I naturally ended up going to their church and began to grow like a spiritual weed. Brenda and I got married immediately when I was at the ripe old age of seventeen.

At that time, the church (in Austin, Texas) had a small group of sincere believers truly seeking God, but was in the beginning process of changing into something very special. Being a basic Baptist, the pastor was being called to something deeper. He began to lead the church on a journey that would result in something akin to the book of Acts. Within a few years, we collectively re-evaluated pretty much every tradition and practice of the common church in the light of the Bible. Some we kept, some we changed, and some we began to practice for the first time. This church was the real deal.

We had uncommon fellowship and a commitment level to that of a family. God began to "clean house" and our once secret sins were being exposed and repented. We began sharing the Gospel—in county jails, retirement homes, concerts, etc—everywhere we could. When visitors walked into our church, it was not uncommon to hear them say that they immediately felt something special. We built a school building for our children and did "co-op home schooling." Purity of life and practical righteousness was the standard. Next the spiritual gifts began to manifest, then the miracles and healings. Like I said, it was akin to the book of Acts. We had become a family and the love and sense of belonging was heavenly. We even changed the church name to Fellowship of the Brethren. The pastor became a "father figure" to me (as he was to others as well) and I found myself trusting a man for the first time in my life.

It was then that God began a long process of healing in my life. I was then long married and in my late twenties and had several more children. Brenda and I ended up having six in all, and yes, the joke is real...we did not have a TV for fourteen years!

The older couples in the church took Brenda and me under their wings and mentored us through biblical teachings. Brenda never really liked the church (at least not as much as I did), and it was never her "first love" as it should have been. I was always the driving spiritual force in our home and relationship. I was a walking, talking, Bible-sharing, Christ-like follower with anyone who would lend me an ear. I was so in love with God and His church that it was hard for me not to share Him with others.

Besides some relational issues with Brenda and common financial struggles, life could not have been better. A normal evening for our family was to eat dinner together, clean up and have evening devotionals and family time. Even if we had another couple over for dinner, or vice versa, we would keep the same pattern as we shared our lives with our extended family church. I was convicted to be the soul bread winner so that Brenda could be home with our children. So I started a painting business that eventually grew to be fairly successful. I had now been a Christian for about ten years and saw only good things in my future. Then everything began to change.

Looking back, I believe that the church pastor and leaders were sincere, but ignorant of the pitfalls of legalism. What we had was so special, unique and powerful, that it went to our heads. Small at first, but subtle changes began to take place in our mindset and application of faith. Our theological doctrine never changed, but our "practilogical" application began to become more and more extreme with each passing month. Before long, evangelism waned off, the healings stopped, mutual acts of service was replaced by micromanaging one another, and the Spirit was replaced by our unspoken but ever-so-enforced list of petty rules for righteousness.

I was never "in the core" and once again found myself seeking approval from my family. We were fast on our way to becoming a sociological cult. In the end, our church wouldn't even allow visitors—there was a three-stage screening process you had to go through before you could even visit. The general atmosphere was one of stringent self righteous holiness, completely void of the Spirit and love. Once again, I couldn't live up to the standard and felt inadequate and weak.

Needless to say, the church imploded and we found ourselves barricaded in our houses, afraid to contact anyone, wondering what had happened. The pastor, my once spiritual father, moved to another city with a few families from "the core" of the church, and I spent the next six months trying to contact him. When I finally reached him, his ultimatum was to distance myself from the other families that I was fellowshipping with, if I wanted to be in contact with him. I knew what this man had said was wrong, and for the first time I went against his counsel. I "flipped the switch" in my head and never talked to him again. That was more than fifteen years ago.

Three families from that church (including mine) began to slowly crawl out of their cocoons and call one another. We eventually formed a church and began home churching together. We recognized the legalism (most of it at least) and set our sights on recovering the good years of our former glory. We were quickly joined by other families and even new people. I had no aspirations of being "the pastor" and so I supported Pastor Cary, a very assertive, longtime friend. Before long, we acquired a facility in town and gave ourselves the name "Living Faith Fellowship." I helped write the church charter and constitution. We quickly grew and a new chapter of life had begun.

I was now in my early thirties with five children. During this time, when we were still home churching, my family, along with another family, also attended a second larger, more structured church in Austin for several years. With its modern more "hip" style atmosphere and teachings, we looked as if we had all just stepped off of the set of Little House on the Prairie, like fish out of water. This was a good church, but a far cry from Christian community and being separate from the world. It was a good experience though. Prior to attending, I had thought I had weeded out all of the legalism, but soon found that I still had work to do.

I remember one of the first services I attended there. I looked to my side during worship and noticed a young man with his hands raised high, eyes closed, and tears streaming down his face. This man reminded me of my early worship experiences when I first surrendered myself to Jesus, and I had two thoughts. The first one was, "I remember when I used to love God that much... but I don't anymore." However, it was followed by a second thought, "Yeah, but God isn't acknowledging his worship anyway. Look at him! He's wearing shorts in church!" Yeah, I had some work to do alright.

I spent the next two years moonlighting at the bigger church where I attended early Sunday services, mid-week home group, and completed leadership training. At the same time, I was also heavily involved in my own church too, attending Sunday services as well as mid-week services. I was ordained as the new believer's elder and wrote an extensive "Christian Faith Study" booklet for the church, and taught it to them as well. I began to feel a deep longing for what I once experienced. I wanted community. I wanted to be a part of a Spirit-led church that functioned as a family. I wanted to see the Holy Spirit work again. I was hungry.

I began studying early church history and discovered an even deeper longing for church as God meant it. This was when my time at the bigger church ended. I spoke with the pastor and as we shook hands, we agreed that I needed to focus on my other church. I was thankful for all that I had learned through that experience. This was about the time when I met Pastor Cary, who was now one of our church leaders, and who was inspired by Rick Warren's book "The Purpose Driven Church". He bought dozens of copies, passed them out, and began nudging the church in the direction of being a seeker sensitive, culturally cool mega church.

This was so different from what I had been reading about—outdated men like Polycarp, Clement of Rome, Tertullian, Justin Martyr and the like. It was also different from what the Holy Spirit had been building in me in the past few years and in our own church charter and visionary statement. Needless to say, we had a problem, and I quickly learned that I was apparently it!

Every one of the other leaders in the church was on board, except for me. I began to "lock horns" with Cary (who I saw as my spiritual peer at best). I was completely vested in our church and planned on growing old with these people while watching our children grow up together. I had no intention of seeking to become what I had just experienced the last two years in the larger church, and was not the least bit moved to change our church into a modern "churchanity" that attracted the crowds but lacked in righteousness and power.

Cary and I really got into it a few times. It seemed that no matter how many church history examples or Bible verses I showed him, he was not open to them. Needless to say, I was not about to cast aside all that God had been revealing to me either. We were at a stalemate. In between the brawls, I met Pastor Dave and his wife, who attended another church and who Brenda and I really liked. I saw a greater maturity in him and his family, which gave us the desire to know them better. I approached him and asked if our families could fellowship with the intent of moving towards a mentoring relationship. Knowing Cary, Pastor Dave understood and agreed. He was the assistant pastor on full-time staff at another church, but like me, he shared the desire for something more.

The tension between Cary and I grew in the following months because we could not come to any agreement. Cary's attitude became more and more contentious. He began to say inappropriate and offensive things that he would later deny and also "quote" me on things that I did not say. Things got so bad that I purchased a mini recorder and would not engage with Cary unless I had it on.

The situation with Cary finally exploded one day when we were helping someone in the church move. Cary became highly emotional, aggressive and loud. Needless to say, I was offended (again). I asked the other elders in the church, as well as Pastor Dave, if they could assist me in going through a Matthew 18 confrontation with Cary, where it states clearly in verses 16-18 that when your brother sins we are to "take one or two others along, so that 'every matter may be established by the testimony of two or three witnesses.' If they still refuse to listen, tell it to the church." The elders agreed.

We met early that week and, to my surprise, Cary had a list of offenses against me. Out of courtesy, I agreed to let him present his issues first. We went into the wee hours of the night as I did my best to reconcile with him where I could. Cary took up the entire night. Finally, about two in the morning, we decided to re-adjourn so I could present my issues against him. That was set for Thursday, but that meeting never took place.

I received a phone call during the week from Cary, who informed me (in a smug voice) that he had been praying and that God had led him not to have the meeting in which I was to confront him. In fact, he was going to bring me before the church to publically hold me accountable. I immediately heard the Spirit tell me that I was going to be put out of the church and that I was not to defend myself. I had a sick feeling inside and just hung up the phone.

That Sunday night, Pastor Cary held a special meeting with the whole church in which he used the 1Corinthians 5-format, and levied 38 charges against me. He gave me the choice to either "Accept them, show remorse and repentance, or be marked as a devise and subversive heretic until God had redirected my feelings." As I sat there and listened to the charges, every last one of them were from situations that were either several years old, resolved, misquoted, inaccurate, or simply made up. Cary did such a good spin job that my wife told me later she didn't even want to ride home with me. I still remember the faces looking back at me as Cary slandered me for over an hour. The meeting ended with my statement that I did not agree with the charges, but that God had told me not to defend myself. That night, I was officially excommunicated.

I almost had a breakdown. I was so emotional at one point I was on the floor in our bedroom, in the fetal position, rocking back and forth making noises. I was so angry, hurt, disappointed, and scared that it paralyzed me. Later that night, I drove back to the church and picked up Cary's six-page paper to use in a rebuttal. I typed up a 30-page document, going through Cary's and my history, and went through every one of his charges and showed them for what they were—presenting supporting evidence from recordings, letters, and witnesses. I called for Cary's repentance and the church for help. The document fell on deaf ears. I was completely isolated. At least my wife and older kids eventually saw the situation for what it was—once they considered the facts. So now we were all out of a church and unable to fellowship with any of our friends we were in relationship with. It was traumatizing.

That week, I contacted Dave. He consoled me and then invited us to his church. Even though I knew the church was not what God had called me to, I had nowhere else to go, so I agreed. Dave told me that he felt he was being called to begin a new church and that we should do it together—since he and I were in such agreement on our views and values. My spirit was lifted after months of being in turmoil. I was so excited about the possibilities.

Dave's family and mine became very close in the following months. My attendance at his church was a mixture of toleration and being grieved. They were doctrinally sound, but far too worldly for my taste and certainly lacked elements of community. Dave, who was on fulltime staff there, agreed with me. I was enduring the experience, waiting for Dave to make a move towards starting a new ministry. I was going to be behind him 100%, but that day never came.

Two years came and went and there was no sign of Dave doing anything. I was growing more and more uneasy about my situation. Brenda and I tried to shield our children from the influence of the worldly children there (including the pastors and elders), but the effect of the church on my children's "attitude" was apparent. Finally, I had had enough. Even though I loved Dave's family, I told him that through prayer, I felt that God had told me to stay until the end of the year and then, "That's it. I am outta here!"

I don't know if he just didn't take me seriously, but at the end of the year when we sat down and told him that we were moving on, he strongly opposed our decision and told us that we were wrong. We left anyway. In the following months, there were several abrasive interactions between us, all pointing to me being in the wrong.

Even though we strove to maintain fellowship time with them after leaving the church, there was a clear problem. Dave and his family blatantly cut us off. After months of avoiding us, I drove to his church office and confronted him. He somewhat agreed, gave some lame excuses, and told me he would call me the next Tuesday. Well, there have been about 625 Tuesdays since then and

I still haven't received that call! Once again, someone I trusted and looked up to burned me and hurt my family. The irony of it all is that not long after this, he himself left the church and joined a sociological cult in Waco.

By the way, it had now been several years since the excommunication with Cary. After denying the situation that he ever "excommunicated me" and dodging any and all wrongdoing, I finally gave up and gave the situation to God. It was then that The Holy Spirit began to work on Cary. He began to have disturbing dreams and difficulty preaching or counseling. He finally initiated the call to me and wanted to reconcile.

At first, Cary tried to downplay the situation, but after several meetings, he finally broke and took responsibility for what he done. He even called a special meeting with all those who were formerly involved years ago and publically confessed. In his own words he said that, "I wanted Brother Reagan to submit or leave. I wanted him under my thumb or out, and he would not do either. So I abused my trust and position. I made up charges against him and brought up things that were either resolved or years old. I thought it would scare him, but the whole thing backfired. Then I tried to cover up what I had done and have been lying to all of you for these past two years." By this time, everyone was in shock, followed by tears of joy—Cary included. He said that he should be removed as the pastor and his fate should be placed in the hands of the elders.

My old friend and I embraced each other and we could not stop crying. Then we all started singing worship songs together.

You could really feel the Spirit's presence there among us. There was complete healing. Brenda and I were asked to return to the church. I knew that invitation would come, but due to the fact that the church was now well on its way to becoming the "modern seeker sensitive" church Cary wanted it to be, I simply could not rejoin.

Our relationship was restored as brothers and sisters and for this, I was extremely blessed. But for obvious reasons, I didn't quite trust him. Although we visited our old church on special occasions, we never returned as regular attendees. The church closed down a few years later and Cary, along with the other elders, began attending other churches—and still are to this day.

My family and I were seriously hurt by the escapades of the past four years. Besides the obvious damage to Brenda and me, our children (who were now mostly teenagers) were deeply damaged by having their friends ripped from their lives—being somewhere just long enough to settle in—then uprooted and relocated once again. It was a very bad time for all of us. Still, through all of this, the vision and calling to a community-based church was stronger than ever. Even though I had a dozen pastors and church leaders telling me over the years that I was being called to start a church, my lack of faith—disguised as humility—kept me trying to force a "square peg in a round hole". I began to write a book (in search of community) on the topic and wanted it more than anything. I was feeling the pressure to find a way to start this community-based church before my children grew up without experiencing what a church like this would feel like, but I could have not been further away from a solution.

Shortly after the fall with Cary, I attempted to get involved with two other churches, but the outcome was the same. At first, they were very interested in my vision and were even asking me to teach them or help implement it in their church, inviting me into the "inner circle" of the leadership. This lasted for months, sometimes years, until eventually it came down to the issue of the pastor needing to make changes himself in order to have what he wanted in his church. That's when I became "the bad guy" and a bur in their saddle.

In various situations, they made it clear that I was no longer welcome. One pastor cussed me out and threatened to beat me up, which I have on tape. The other pastor was highly offended because he found out that I recorded him when he called me to backbite another brother in the church as he tried to influence me to "take his side." I made a transcript and gave it to the brother he was backbiting and asked him if (considering my past) he would leave me out of the situation, but that I would be praying for peace between them. Well, wouldn't you know it? The very next day, I got a call from this pastor telling me that he did not say the things I reported him saying.

When he called me, I put him on speakerphone for my wife to hear. He kept insisting that I misrepresented him and that I was wrong for recording him. He was unmoved by my offer to play the recording so he could hear it for himself. Instead, he gave ultimatums to either show up at his house with the tapes in one hand and my apology in the other, or I was not welcome to come back to his church. Hearing those words, Brenda broke out crying. She knew that it had happened again.

I told this pastor that the reason I recorded him in the first place was not only because he was showing himself to be untrustworthy in several other situations, but also because I was warned he was calling people in the church backbiting the other brother he had a problem with. I told him I didn't do anything wrong and that maybe he should be more concerned with his own actions rather than with the one who caught him! Well, that went over like a lead balloon and I was told never to come back. Again.

I hung up the phone and hugged Brenda. As I opened the door to get her some tissues, I caught my 16-year-old son, Colton—with his ear firmly planted against the door—eavesdropping, so I smacked him on the head. Then I noticed the tears in his eyes.

I started to yell at him but before I could say anything, Colton blurted out, "I know I shouldn't have been listening, Dad, but I'm glad I did. All along I thought you were the problem in these churches, but now I know that it's not you. That it was never you!" He told me that if I would have told him Brother Bob had said the things he heard him say, he wouldn't have believed me. Then the real backbreaker came.

My son informed me that Bob had talked with him weeks before and told him he thought we might be leaving the church soon, and if that happened, he could come and live with him as soon as he turned 17! Colton said he would have done it, too, had he not heard the conversation for himself. This man was not only dividing the church, he was dividing my family—by trying to steal my own son away from me, as well.

Well, that was it. I called a family meeting and we all decided that we had had it with the church. All churches, in fact. We decided to take a "sabbatical" from going anywhere for a while. The past six years had left us all very hurt and confused, and also extremely angry that we had lost our bearings. Clearly, God's leaders had made us stumble, and turned a healthy Christian family into a ball of contempt.

Isolated and hurt, we were exactly where Satan wanted us. We now had our newest edition, our sixth child, Christina, who was born with Down's syndrome and two holes in her heart. Brenda and I, and even our other kids, spent all that we had in every sense caring for little Tina around the clock. It was exhausting. Within two months of our decision to "take a break", Brenda and I began to fight. The pressures of our already strained life could not handle the added weight.

One day I came home to find Brenda packing. She said that our home was totally Godless (which it was), and that she was going to take the kids and go live with a wealthy Christian family we knew. I strongly disagreed and told her that our home was the only stability our kids had left and that we were not going to take that away from them. "If you want to get away from me that bad, then I'll just leave." Truth be told, this was the excuse my flesh was waiting for.

I "moved out" and started sleeping in the guest room above a gym belonging to a church where I once had a basketball ministry—sneaking in at night and leaving in the early morning—

before anyone got there. I would go to work during the day, and at night I would go to the house, eat dinner with the kids, fight with Brenda, and leave. This lasted for weeks until one day I completely snapped.

I was driving through Austin and glanced over at this strip club called the Yellow Rose. In my mind I said, "F this" and I pulled in. I had officially given up on life. There, I met a young girl who I ended up moving in with for a short time. She introduced me to a world that I had never known. Before long, I was going out clubbing and drinking three to four times a week. I also met her friends who were pretty much all interested in me as well. You can fill in the blanks, but needless to say, I was spiritually AWOL and officially backsliding.

I tried a few drugs once or twice, but that wasn't really my thing. I suppose, due to my past of being rejected as a person most of my childhood, and also being rejected by Brenda (sexually) for most of our marriage, my "drug" was the attention I was getting from these young girls. I was already into fitness, but now I really turned it up. I even changed my wardrobe.

By this time, I was barely going home but once a week or so. My new lifestyle was providing me with pressure-free fun—an escape from my former life. It's like I completely abandoned Brenda, my children, and what I once called my home. I was clearly out of my mind and just as the Lord says in John 8:34, I quickly became a slave of the sin I practiced.

I still had my painting company, but it wasn't exempt from my neglect either. Before long I began to lose long-held contracts.

In addition to my new life, I was still paying all the bills for my "home" as well. This went on for close to a year. I was completely numb towards anything I once knew. All I could think about was the next party with my new friends.

By this time, my older children were in their late teens and I had no idea what they were doing or how Brenda was doing for that matter, nor would my new mentality and lifestyle afford me to care. That all changed when, one day, I got a call from my son.

Colton called me and told me that I needed to come home. He said his mom was having a nervous breakdown and that he was really worried about her. So I went to the house. There I found the woman I loved sitting on the back porch. Still in her pajamas in the middle of the day, she was staring out into the field—as she rocked back and forth with a glass of wine in one hand and a cigarette in the other. I could tell that she had not shaved or showered in days, if not weeks. My children were there, but not really, if you know what I mean. Isolated as well, their trust had been broken, their lives completely uprooted from all that was good and everything they had ever known. As hard as my heart was, it was all too much to ignore. I got Brenda in the shower and helped her get cleaned up.

The whole situation brought a certain amount of sobriety to me, at least enough to reconsider my situation. I told Benda I felt that I needed to come back home and focus on the family and my business. I also said that I had been going out and that I was not ready to walk with the Lord yet, but I was going to stop going out. Things could have taken a turn for the better, but just the opposite happened.

To my surprise, she told me that all sounded good, except for the not going out part. “You’ve been having all the fun,” she said. “I want you to take me out to have some fun, too.” Well, that sure sounded good to me. The day was Thursday. Thursday night I always went to a certain club, so I told her about it and she could not have gotten ready sooner.

That’s when I had to break it to her—that I was not still stowing away at the gym. I told her about where I was staying, but lied to her about my relations with this girl. I had to tell her about my new “residence” because we needed to go back to Roxanne’s house to get my clothes. When we got to the house, Roxanne was there and I told her that I was moving out. I was never her “boyfriend” and she was fine with that. In fact, she wanted to go out with us! I left this completely up to my wife. Brenda and Roxanne were getting along fine (behold the power of wine) and so we all headed to the club.

I never could have imagined the following events in a thousand years, and I will be discreet here, but the short of it all is that we all ended up together. Now I was in a sinners’ paradise. I could have my cake and eat it, too. Brenda and I were both going out three to four times a week, as we were both addicted to sin—while abandoning the kids alone at the house.

This lasted for about six months. By this time, my business was all but extinct due to neglect. I had no contracts left and only my son was working for me off and on. Brenda came to me one day out, of the blue, and told me that we needed ten thousand dollars... now! "For what?" I asked. "To keep ourselves off the streets", was her response.

We sat down and went over the bills and to my shock we were two to three months behind in everything. We had gone through all our savings and had almost nothing coming in. Literally, in less than a month, we were going to be without power, phone, gas, insurance, and water. But none of this really mattered because we were going to be out of our house as well! She said that she had to borrow money from her father last month—just to buy food.

I got a shot of reality and told her that I was done going out (as often anyway) and I was going to refocus on what was left of my business. I had one last big job coming up. I was going to put my "whites" back on, grab my son and a few Hispanic workers and hit it hard. I was not about to go back to being dirt poor and living hand to mouth much less have my family on the streets.

The next day, I had Brenda call all the creditors and ask for a few more weeks—promising to pay them soon. I was dead set on rebuilding my business. I drove out to the jobsite, a new construction multi-million dollar residence. My former crew had already completed the exterior and the boat dock and we were waiting for the interior which paid about thirty thousand—more than enough to get us out of this hole.

To my dismay, there were paint samples on the interior and they were not mine. I called the builder who reluctantly told me that I had lost the job! He apologized and said that it had nothing to do with me, but that the homeowner hired an interior decorator that was influencing them to use her own contractors. He said that he would use me "on the next one." As I hung up the phone, I knew that there wasn't going to be a "next one." The thought immediately came. I had never even considered anything of the sort before, but I was desperate. I was going to "rob a bank."

As crazy as the notion was, it seemed to be my only option. So just like that I began to plan a robbery. I don't need to go into details on the following activity, but needless to say, I started robbing banks. Absolute insanity for a normal person, but for someone with my background and history, it was not believable. I employed the military mentality my second stepfather instilled in me along with the "switch" to turn off my emotions, and there I was... a bank robber!

We paid our bills and my heart became even harder, going out as much as I (we) could without even the thought of my former business (which was by this time officially gone). By this time, I had not gone to church, prayed, or done anything remotely spiritual in about two years. I never quit believing in God, and wasn't even mad at Him—I was playing the role of the prodigal son.

I suppose that I would have continued down that path until "whenever." I really don't know, nor did I think much about it, but my Father had not forgotten about me and had a plan to get me back with Him. Little did I know, but I would soon be given that opportunity although it would come at an extremely high cost. By this time, our children were cold towards us—hurting and looking for a way out of their situation.

Brenda and I were growing apart as she was finding it hard to keep up with me. She decided to go to Wisconsin with the kids for a vacation. Everyone went except our oldest daughter, Faith, who stayed back with me. Brenda was supposed to be gone for a week, but that turned into more than a month.

During that time, unbeknownst to either of us, we were both unfaithful to one another (as if that really mattered anymore). I didn't plan it that way. In fact, I had arranged a "baby sitter" to keep me in line. This guy was no help at all and was instead encouraging me to get together with other women. I was completely out of control in every way and had no way out, but God still loved me and, in spite of myself, He already had a plan in motion to deliver me.

The last robbery I pulled was three months ago. The following day, the police arrested some guy for doing it. I felt bad, but what could I do? Turn myself in? I don't think so. I was in the clear for sure, or so I thought.

I went to "work" the next day... meaning my new girlfriend's house. That evening I was in a bar shooting pool with her and freaking out about what I was going to do about my screwed up situation. A short time later, the manager came over and told me that someone had wrecked my truck in the parking lot and he wanted me to come outside. The man was an undercover F.B.I. agent who had about six of his friends waiting to greet me.

As soon as I walked out, they greeted me with a hard push, a knee in the back, and Glock 9mm pistols with pretty laser sites. As I lay there, I had two thoughts; the first was that my life was over, the second thought was, "how in the heck did they catch me?"

They took me to the filthiest place I had ever been—the violent section of the county jail. The "food" was barely consumable. At the same time, the police and detectives were tearing apart the house. Brenda said that when they left, she couldn't even see the floors. She took them to the storage unit where I had a safe containing all the money. They took that and just about anything else they wanted—related to the crime or not. She also willingly gave them the new Yukon we had purchased with stolen money still valued at $30 grand.

Brenda came to visit me for the first time, and wouldn't you know it, my new girlfriend was there. As they sat next to each other and chatted, it wasn't long until they figured out that they were both there to see the same man. Like the word says in Numbers 32:23, "be sure that your sins will find you out." As I sat there in black and white stripes behind the dirty Plexiglas, Brenda confronted me immediately. What could I say? I was at the end of my rope. It was all over. Everything! My wife told me we would worry about it later and that we had more pressing issues to focus on, like getting a lawyer. About a month later she retained one for me. In talking to him, I started to realize very quickly just how much all this would cost me in the end—not only the amount of money, but my time behind bars.

I was immediately informed that I was looking at more than seventy years and that the prosecutor was offering me forty years in a plea agreement. I was dumbfounded. "They must have me confused with someone else. I robbed a few banks. I didn't kill anyone!" But it was me they were referring to and I was indicted on two bank robberies and three gun charges.

The Federal sentencing guidelines call for seven years for the first count, 25 years for the second, and another 25 years for the third count, all to be stacked on top of one another—and then whatever I would get sentenced for the robberies. So I was looking at a minimum of 57 years (plus the robberies) for my first offense ever. I began to believe and had the very realistic fear that I was going to die in prison.

Needless to say, I didn't accept the prosecutor's generous offer. Besides the ton of pressure hanging over my head, I began to sober up (mentally) and realized what an idiot I had been. I truly missed my wife and children. I sent out many wrinkled letters previously soaked by my tears. I was broken, and that's when God's faint but steady calling began to come through. I was now in a 24-man tank (concrete box) 23 hours a day. They would let us out (to another concrete box) for recreation one hour a day.

In my new "home", there was a group of guys meeting daily, trying to study the Bible. I saw them but purposely avoided talking with them about anything spiritual. No one knew of my history, but eventually I got caught. I was sitting next to them as they were debating over a certain passage and one of them asked me if I knew what it meant. I gave the shortest answer I could and you should have seen their faces light up. Then they asked me another question, and another, and another. God's word has power and, even reluctantly discussing it, was the added nudge I needed to help my heart find its way back to God.

Riddled with guilt, shame and pride, I was avoiding the

Father, but His love finally broke through. I, as the prodigal son, had spent all I had and found myself in the "pigpen" of my own making, crying out for the love and care I once knew in my Father. I wanted to go back home where I knew I belonged all along.

Slowly, but surely, I went through a series of breakdowns. It was the most painful and yet most cleansing time I had ever experienced... even more than when I first gave my life to Christ. How so? Because I actually sinned more after knowing the truth than I did before! There was no claim of ignorance. I knew exactly what I was doing and that it was wrong. I just didn't care.

My heart had been completely hardened through the deceitfulness of sin, but now it was being broken, and it was not an easy process. I now hated and despised the life I had been living. It disgusted me. As I repented more and more each day, I began to rediscover God's presence and feel His joy. I completely recommitted myself back to God. I then could feel His forgiveness and acceptance once more.

I was soon leading the Bible group that grew to almost half of the tank. In the next few months, many were touched by God and committed themselves to Him. In the whole facility, our tank was known as the "Christian tank." I began to seek reconciliation with Brenda and the kids— working to somehow rebuild and salvage as much as I could. It was a bittersweet time.

About this time, I found out how they caught me. Looking back, I can clearly see the fingerprints of God in it all. I had a friend named Elton who, strangely enough, I had helped lead to the Lord through the basketball ministry. I invested a lot of time and resources in this young man. We took him into our home for several months and I even baptized him. Unfortunately, he started to backslide about the same time I did.

We both knew of our "condition" and avoided each other for at least a year. It's a story in and of itself, and looking back is somewhat comical, but the short of it is that I got Elton involved in my robberies to help him, and it was through him that I got caught. He led the police right to himself, and when he was questioned, he gave them a 70-minute statement against me telling them everything he thought they might want to know... and then some. He thought if he cooperated, they were going to let him go. Wrong!

The details of why and how I got Elton involved and then how badly he "messed things up" was so bizarre that it's clear to me God arranged for that to happen in order to get me caught...to begin the process of breaking me and bringing me back to Him. I wish there could have been another way, but in all honesty, I was so far gone that outside of all this, I probably would have never come back to Him on my own.

About four months into my case, my attorney came with "great" news. He said that the prosecutor was going to drop two of the gun charges if I plead guilty to one of them. There was no mention of threatening Benda with prosecution at this time. The problem with the whole deal was that I didn't use a real gun in the robbery. I had two pistols... one was an antique and one I recently bought because I was in the process of taking a "concealed and carry course". I took both of them to a gun shop to have the antique gun appraised. They were both in a single gun case locked in the tool box on my truck up until I was arrested. The crazy thing is that months after my arrest, I discovered that the Feds were still looking for my pistols. I thought they had them all along. I called Brenda and she said that they had to pry open my toolbox when I was arrested. So where were my pistols?

After thinking about it, I concluded that there was only one possible theory. Prior to the bank robbery, I was with a group of friends having a tail gate party and I sat on my tool box. It "popped" and I noticed that the latches on the box were bent up. I bent them back and tried to open it, but I couldn't. I even bent the key in the latch. Later that week I went back to where I had recently bought the $350.00 industrial toolbox. My salesman took my truck in the back and they tried to get into it themselves, but they were unsuccessful. I was told that they were going to order new latches for me and just drill out the old ones and replace them with the new ones.

It was over a month before I got the call and I procrastinated. I didn't go back for another two months, even though they called me several times. I never got back into my tool box. The Feds were the first ones to get into it since I had had it repaired, and they had to use a crow bar. They never did find the guns, yet all this time, I thought they had them. But evidently and unbeknownst to me, my tool box had been robbed at some point. When I sat on it that day and it popped, it was already damaged and I believe that was when the pistols were stolen. Prior to the robbery, I couldn't have used my real guns because I didn't have access to them. As far as

I knew, they were still locked up in my broken tool box.

To this day, the Feds still do not have my pistols, 12 years later. They have no physical evidence—which was probably why the prosecutor was willing to drop two of the gun charges if I plead guilty to one. By the way, there is a big difference between using a real loaded firearm and a pellet pistol... about 5 ½ years difference. Well, I wasn't about to plead guilty to something I was not. So I informed my attorney that I was not going to plead guilty and to begin preparations to move towards a trial to prove my innocence of the gun charge. He told me I was crazy to risk it and that I should just plead guilty.

Almost a month passed. By this time, Brenda had purchased a steel pellet pistol similar to the one I used. I told my son to drill out the barrel and paint it matte black. In my work shed was the drill with the drill bit still in it from me working on the other pellet pistol.

We were close to jury selection and I felt good moving forward with the trial. I was pretty confident that they couldn't indict me on the gun charge. On the big robbery I pulled, I had dressed in a police uniform and convinced the teller (just opening up the bank) that I was there to prevent a robbery. She held the door open for me and about ten minutes later, I left with all the money they had in the vault. Everything I had was fake; the police shirt, police hat, belt, badge, and the pistol. I was sure that I would beat the gun charge and that the government had no real evidence as to me using a real gun. Several letters were exchanged between me and my lawyer working on our trial strategy as we were close to beginning.

Then it happened. I got a surprise visit from my attorney on a Sunday afternoon of all times. He told me that he received a call from the prosecutor and that it was bad news. He said the prosecutor had told him that if I took them to trial, she would indict Brenda, have her arrested, and then call GPS. Then our children would be spread out all over in foster homes. The prosecutor's message was, "Go ahead and take us to trial, but I will personally make sure that your client won't have a family when he gets out!" My lawyer said that the prosecutor was not bluffing this time and that I had until Wednesday that week to make up my mind, because Brenda would be indicted by Friday if I didn't plead guilty.

I had been in the system long enough to know that this sort of activity was not uncommon to some prosecutors, and although it was unethical and even illegal, it was just another loophole—so they could get away with it. My attorney had written me several letters prior, clearly voicing his opinion of the prosecutor's actions: "I truly believe that the prosecutor trying to force you into pleading guilty by threatening your wife is despicable." Another letter said, "The prosecutor brought up your wife again. The prosecutor once again offered you to plead to all charges in exchange for your wife's freedom." So what was I to do?

Soon thereafter, I found myself signing a piece of paper and standing before a judge lying through my teeth. One of the things judges always ask the defendant is, "Are you pleading guilty for no other reason than you are guilty, and has anyone made any promises or threats against you?" When I was asked this, I just stood there in silence for what seemed like minutes. My attorney nudged me several times to get me to respond—to lie. And so I did. I lied— concerning my guilt—as a result of the prosecutor's "threats" and the ineffective assistance of my attorney, who should have notified the court from the very beginning.

I was sentenced to eight years for the robberies and seven for the gun charge—about fifteen in all. The prosecutor also tried to get me charged with "kidnapping", claiming that I forced the teller to walk a few feet into the bank (even though anyone who would take the time to watch the tapes would see that she actually held the door open for me). But thankfully the judge shot down her attempt.

I was then warned by the judge that I could appeal if I wanted to, but he pointed out that he had been easy on me and that it would not go well for me if I tried to appeal. I assume that statement was in complete ignorance of the facts. As far as I know, all that went down (with the prosecutor) was done "under the table" without the court's knowledge. This was what makes this sort of thing illegal and corrupts the system.

Almost two years of the eight was a result of me not getting my "acceptance for responsibility." Even though the Feds had all the money, I was accused of hiding some of it (about 20 to 30 thousand). I knew that the reported amount of money was shorter than what was in the safe, (that only I had access to), but I didn't know how or why. I found out later that when the local detective and his assistant drove Brenda to the interior climate-controlled storage unit where the safe was kept, after they opened up the door and saw the safe, with key in hand, they made her go unescorted back outside to their car and wait so they could "examine the evidence." I'll give you three guesses where the missing money went.

If I had my own money to pay the missing amount, I would do it in a heartbeat. Who thinks that two years of their life is not worth 20 to 30 thousand dollars? The notion is ridiculous. So from my perspective, I am not only being incarcerated for an additional seven years for the bogus gun charge (and not getting the 2 or 3 points off for acceptance), but I even have to pay back the missing 20 to 30 thousand in addition to another 30 thousand from the Yukon they confiscated but didn't credit against my restitution.

After I was sentenced, I was sent to a Federal Prison in Texas to do my time. It's a low security facility and actually quite nice. I didn't care what it looked like. I was just elated that I was going to be close to my family so we could see each other during visitation. When I got there, everyone else on the bus was released to the compound, but I was put in the "special housing unit"... what we call the SHU, or the hole.

My case manager came the next day and told me that they were going to ship me out to a medium security because "they didn't house people like me there." I tried to tell him he had nothing to worry about, but my plea fell on deaf ears. The "hole" was much like the county jails I had been in except for being all alone in a small room. The window was even painted black. I spent the night in prayer, pleading with God to let me stay there close to my family.

The next morning, I woke to the sound of birds chirping outside the window. I couldn't see them, but just the sound moved me to tears. "Birds!" I said to myself. In the various concrete boxes I had been in, I had not heard them in six months. It sounds silly, but when a man has been stripped from everything and broken to a point of nothingness, even the smallest of things have tremendous impact and meaning. I was convinced that God had arranged for me to be designated here close to my family and this case manager, who didn't know me from Adam, was trying to get me shipped out. I was determined not to eat until God had the victory. I wasn't going to eat unless it was in the chow hall right there in that Texas Federal Prison. Of course I didn't tell them that. It was between me and my God. "You can let me starve to death if You want Lord, but I'm not going to eat until Your will is done."

Maybe I was crazy, but six days later, my case manager came and told me that they were going to let me out on a probationary basis. So on the seventh day (the day of completion from when God formed the earth and all that it contains), they let me out and I ate my breakfast right in the chow hall. I came in the system weighing 210 pounds of muscle and was now down to 165.

I was elated to find the prison filled with many sincere believers. I was welcomed by the Christian brothers and quickly got involved in the church. In the following years, I helped to pioneer the vision for unit Bible groups which eventually grew to about 24 groups of five to ten men. I learned to play the guitar and became the worship leader. In all, I really committed myself to further God's kingdom in any way that I could.

Most importantly, I focused on rebuilding my relationship and trust with my family—especially Brenda. By this time we had both confessed our unfaithfulness, forgave each other and had restored our marriage. The first visit we all were really a mess. The allergies must have been extremely high that day as they started acting up as soon as I laid eyes on them (tough convicts never cry... we get allergies). We must have looked like walking water works.

God had been healing me and He was now working on my family as I begged for their forgiveness. The kids were slow to trust at first, but came along when they saw the father they once knew. We were being restored.

As I began to learn more about the law, I decided to begin the appeal process. I believed that the letters from my lawyer would be more than enough evidence to open up my case again so I could tell my side of the story—the truth the court has never heard as of yet. I have spent over five years in the appellate system. To my complete shock and disappointment, and in spite of Supreme Court rulings in cases identical to mine, every appeal has been denied. I even submitted it to the Supreme Court who didn't even bother to look at it. Responding to a 20-page brief, their response was: "Your request for a certiorari has been denied." It was rubberstamped by the clerk. So needless to say, I am writing this story from my prison cell. I still have a few irons in the fire, but for now, my release date is still 2018.

Over the years, I have really struggled with what I feel to be a failure of the system and violations of my constitutional rights.

I certainly know that I was completely wrong in committing the bank robberies, and that I (and anyone else who commits a crime) deserve to be punished. However, maybe I am old fashioned, but I still believe that "two wrongs don't make a right".

There is a reason that America has five times the incarceration rate of any other country on earth. The Federal system is 150% overcrowded at about 220 thousand inmates and is costing taxpayers about eight billion dollars annually. Every year, it is increased by an additional six to eight thousand. As one Senator put it, "Either, we are the most evil people on the face of the earth, or there is something very wrong with our system."

When my final appeal was denied, I was so stressed out that, in spite of my stringent diet and exercise regimen, I developed high blood pressure for over a year. Very high blood pressure... like 185 over 120! That is stage-three hypertension. Medical sent me out to a cardiologist and spent thousands of tax payer's dollars on tests, revealing that there was nothing physically wrong with me. It was then that I knew (beyond denial) that I was not trusting in God.

I was convicted by the Spirit and needed to grow and mature in my ability to really trust in Him and be abandoned to His will. After all, if God wanted me out, wouldn't I be? Did I really trust that He was in control? I wrestled with this for a while and even though I should have been out years ago, I eventually abandoned myself to His will. I know He is using me to reach men in here and further His kingdom behind these walls, and if this is where He wants me for now, then I'm okay with that. I don't like it, but I'll submit to it for as long as He wills. When I released my situation to God, my blood pressure leveled out and returned back to normal. Go figure.

Brenda was with me for three years after my arrest, but never really re-solidified her relationship with God. She waffled back and forth until she finally fell for good. In our last visit she told me, "I don't have a relationship with the Lord and I'm tired of trying. I'm going to start going out again. I'm not saying that I'm going to be unfaithful to you, Ray, but I'm not going to make any promises either."

I spent the next hour or so trying to talk some sense into her, but she had already made up her mind. That was on a Thursday. I was heavy hearted and was really in prayer for her. I woke the next morning about 3am sick to my stomach. I could clearly feel her having sex with someone. I spent the next three hours crying and praying until the officer unlocked the door.

I got up and went into the showers, and then fell to my knees sobbing. I called the house as soon as they turned on the phones and one of my daughters answered. "Let me talk to Mommy, honey." But my daughter was quick to inform me, "She's not here, Dad. We're really worried about her. She went out last night and hasn't come home yet." I assured them all that their mom was okay and that she would be home soon. I knew then that our marriage was over. It took three additional years, but I finally got the divorce papers in the mail. It was the end of a 27-year relationship.

Brenda never blamed me or tried to point her finger at me for the decisions she had chosen. Once I repented and came back to God, I had truly given it my all to reconcile, and she knew that. I'm proud to say that in the three years of visits, there's not one thing I said that I wish I had not, and there's nothing that I didn't say that I wish I had. God really gave me a lot of grace and maturity during this time. I'm glad and thankful for several reasons.

I can look my children in their eyes and tell them that I truly did everything possible to stay with their mother and to make it work. I made terrible decisions that wrecked all of our lives, and I will live with those consequences for the rest of my life, but God is a God of second chances. He teaches us that no matter how far we fall, we can reach out to Him and be restored and finish strong in His power. That's all I can hope for.

There isn't a day that goes by that I wish I had not gone down the path I did. In those few short years of turning away from God, I had lost what took 20 years to build, and that was before I put myself in prison! The most difficult thing I have struggled with is forgiving myself. All I can do is make sure that I never, for any reason, turn away from following Christ again. I want to seek His will for my life and walk in His forgiveness and strength forever.

During this time, God had restored the vision for a community church and also given me a vision for a unique prison ministry—my plan is to start both. I have also written (and will try to publish) several books, a study guide, and about 60 songs which I have written. I am also currently in the process of taking college Bible courses. (You have them to thank for requiring me to write this testimony). I don't know exactly how all of this will pan out, but

I am very excited about getting my Father's business as soon as I can—on the other side of the fence.

I want nothing more than to work for Him fulltime furthering His kingdom. That day is coming. My children will be my first priority. They need my help and seem to be stuck in spiritual limbo land. My ability to minister to them is extremely limited in here, but they will be my number one focus when I get out. Somewhere in all this, I need to rebuild my financial life as well.

My plate is as full as it can get, but I trust my Lord Jesus to work it all out in His own way. More than ever before, I am deeply in love with Him and eternally grateful for all He has done, all He is doing now, and all He has yet to do. This was certainly not "Plan A" but I believe He will make "beauty from ashes and give the oil of joy for mourning" (Isaiah 61:3). He will "restore the years that the locust have eaten" (Joel 2:25). He is my all in all and I am His.

Many have asked me, "How?" How does one go from being a committed believer, Bible teacher and family man to an adulterating bank robber? Well, I have found the answer to that. Like the saying goes, "How do you eat an elephant? One small bite at a time." In that lies your answer—one small compromise at a time. I believe that there is a lesson in my story for all of us. I have come to believe that, given the right set of circumstances, we are all capable of just about anything—one small compromise at a time.

If you don't believe that, I understand. I once thought the same way. Be sure of one thing though, sin will take you further than you ever wanted to go, keep you there longer than you ever wanted to stay, and cost you more than you ever wanted to pay. I knew this before in my mind, but now I know it in my heart. I have a new understanding of the passage that warns us all, "if any man thinks he stands, take heed lest ye fall" (1Corinthians 10:12).

I was "afflicted in every way, but not crushed; perplexed, but not despairing; persecuted, but not forsaken; struck down, but not destroyed" (2Corinthians 4:8-9). My God snatched me from the hands of Satan. His grace has saved me more times than I can count. I am a walking testimony. To Him be the glory forever.

From Sinner Jew to Savior Jesus

I was raised in a fairly stable Jewish home. I went to a Hebrew School and had a Bat Mitzvah when I was 13. My family celebrated all the Jewish holidays and kept Kosher but, after 18 years in the faith, I couldn't tell you five things I learned about God.

In 1973, my first year in college, I met a man who I cared for deeply. I thought he would make a good husband and that we would spend the rest our lives together. He was kind and attentive and he treated me with respect. We fell in love and married a year later. After college, we started our family. We had three amazing children together and everything was exactly what I hoped it would be—a big home, good income, and a very rewarding life. It wasn't perfect, but it was good. I was happy and secure, and I put all my trust in my husband, in our children, in our home, and in our money. What else did I need?

We went along with little conflict. I was working as a nurse on the psychiatric floor of a hospital, and it was there that I met Terri for the first time. She was unlike anyone I had ever known. She ignited love and had this glow about her. She also had this amazing, almost unconditional love for even the most unlovely patients. I was very drawn to her and desperately wanted to have what she had. If it came in a bottle, I would buy it. If it was injected, I would be its subject. If it was taught, I would be its most attentive pupil.

We soon became friends and she started sharing with me what it was that made her different. It wasn't bought, injected, or taught. It was Jesus. Well, that wouldn't work for me. I was Jewish—and Jews don't do Jesus. We became good friends anyway and she gently shared her faith as she poured out Christ-like love, but I kept it at arm's length. I just couldn't go there.

Then one day in May 1996, after 21 years of marriage, family, and security, my husband came home from work and announced that he didn't want to be married to me anymore. Just like that, without the slightest remorse, he told me that he had found someone else and that he wanted to be with her. He said he didn't love me anymore. In fact, he informed me that he had never loved me! I was so taken aback that I could barely move. Was he joking? How could this be?

In an instant my whole world came crashing down. Everything I had built my future on was suddenly gone—my husband, my house, my family, my self esteem. With a snap of a finger the life I had known disappeared into a puff of black smoke, as if it had never been. I was beyond devastated. I suddenly realized that the 21 years of marriage which I had experienced were vastly different from his 21-year experience. He was all I needed and, though it wasn't perfect, I thought we were doing fairly well. However, all I had ever been to him was a fill-in—someone to take care of his needs, his home and his children—until something better came along.

I was angry and very hurt, which sent me into a deep depression. It felt as if I had been robbed all those years we had spent together; years that I could have been with someone else who loved me. On the other hand, it brought to light why I was always unable to fully connect to my husband. No matter how hard I tried reaching out to him, he never let me "in". I realize now that he never wanted me "in" because his plans for us were not permanent.

I thought him a coward, knowing from the beginning that he didn't love me, and yet allowing the marriage to continue for so long—until he was done with me. I also found out that the woman he was seeing wasn't even his first attempt at having an affair. There had been several others along the way who he had tried to seduce. It was all so humiliating and disjointing as I tried to reconcile—in my mind and in my heart—what had happened.

It was as if my whole life had been one cruel lie which I wasn't even privy to until 21 years later. I felt foolish and used—it was a horrible time. In an effort to have some kind of control, I started a vastly-reduced dietary intake. As I lost weight, I felt powerful in that realm if nowhere else. I quickly became anorexic with a weight of under 100 pounds. Through my eyes, I thought I looked amazing, but in reality I looked very sickly. When my family saw me, they were horrified. They felt helpless and were terrified that I would die. At this point, I am not even sure I cared if I did. It was that bad.

I quickly went down into the deepest, darkest pit you could ever imagine. There was no escape. I was depressed, rejected and filled with an overwhelming amount of pain that I had never experienced before. I could not imagine how I could live in this world any longer. What would be the reason? Everything I had was gone.

Eventually, I stopped eating altogether and stayed in my gloomy bedroom alone, with the door closed and the shades drawn for days and weeks on end. My faith was gone. My hope destroyed. Was this what life was going to be for me now? If so, I wanted out.

My dear friend Terri came to visit me every day. It was so like her. She had a heart of pure gold and it shined from the inside out. I didn't care about her Christian roots. I was just grateful to have someone who truly cared. She sat with me and wiped my tears. She reached out to me with love and comfort. She spent hours with me listening to my pain. She never complained. She just listened. Terri ministered to my broken heart and shattered spirit.

During this time she talked to me about Jesus and encouraged me to trust Him as my Savior. I wanted to, but I felt I just could not do it yet. Yes, I was Jewish, but that wasn't the real reason I felt I couldn't receive Christ. I was a sinner—a sinner with a very dark secret sin which I had never shared with anyone before.

Back in 1974, shortly after my marriage, I had become inconveniently pregnant. A baby just did not fit into the plans my husband and I had at the time. We were just starting off; we had no money and my husband still had to finish school—it was just bad timing. I did what many other women have chosen to do in that same situation. I had an abortion. Problem solved.

But now, here was Jesus. How could I come face to face with God now? I took my own child's life! I was flooded with guilt. I felt ashamed and unworthy of forgiveness. If I believed in Jesus then I would have to face my sin. I would have to feel the pain of what I had done to my child. It was the hardest thing I had ever done, but I needed to finally be freed from the shame and pain.

I got on my knees and, with tears and trembling, I cried out to Jesus to forgive me and come into my heart. And He did! I felt Him enter my spirit. It was so very, very real and powerful and true. I felt the change inside immediately. I felt forgiven. I knew I was saved, and I knew my life was now in His hands. I had real hope for the first time since my husband had walked out of our marriage.

The person who got up off her knees was not the same as the one who went down. I felt the difference. People who saw me saw the difference. I was a sinner, but I was forgiven. I finally had what Terri had—the love of Christ. And it was beautiful.

Isaiah 43:18-19 "Remember not the former things, nor consider the things of old. Behold, I am doing a new thing; now it springs forth, do you not perceive it? I will make a way in the desert and rivers in the dry land."

I wished I could stand before you today and say that I grew in Christ and followed Him on a pure path and in righteousness—that it was all smooth sailing, happy and easy—but that would add more lying to my litany of sins. According to 1Peter 5:8 "Your adversary the devil prowls around like a roaring lion, seeking someone to devour…" and he was out to devour me. I had accepted Jesus into my life, and that was real, but so were the circumstances and wreckage of my life.

I was still sad and lonely, and still felt extremely rejected, filled with the need to have something or someone. The enemy still had a grip on my life, and I was a baby in my faith-walk with Christ. So instead of turning to Christ to meet my needs, I turned to Terri. We ended up engaged in a homosexual relationship. She filled that need in me—that void, that hole. I felt loved again. But I also knew it was very wrong. And so did Terri! I had not realized until later that Terri had been suffering a battle of her own in her marriage and was desperately struggling to get through it. We leaned on each other for support and gave into our temptations.

Little did either of us know how strong the pull of temptation could be when you're too distraught to think straight. Satan slithered about waiting to pounce. Then, when we were at our weakest, he subtlety slipped past all the morals and values we had been taught on his way to kill, steal and destroy us both (John 10:10).

The relationship I had with Terri lasted for several years, but try as I might I could not reconcile my behavior with my new faith in Christ. I felt awful, laden with guilt. All around I watched as Terri's world came crashing down. She told her husband about the relationship because he sensed something was going on. He would listen to our phone calls, scrutinize any written notes, interrogate her, and spy on her. Finally she admitted to him that our relationship had become sexual.

We both knew we were filling our lives with immoral sin and lust. I continued to read the Bible. I needed more than what even Terri could give. Romans 6:12-13 says, "Let not sin reign in your mortal bodies, to make you obey their passions. Do not present your members to sin as instruments for unrighteousness, but present yourselves to God as those who have been brought from death to life and your members to God as instruments for righteousness. For sin will have no dominion over you since you are not under law but under grace."

As I learned more and more about God and grew closer to Him, I became increasingly broken and convicted that our relationship was wrong, and I had to get out. By this time we had ended the sexual aspect, but we still clung to each other emotionally. We thought we could repent of our sexual sin (which we did), but still keep a friendship. How deeply we were deceived. My life was really focused more on her than it was on Christ. And it wasn't going well. I needed Christ to be my Savior, not Terri.

Her husband was (understandably) furious and did everything he could think of to make it stop. I see now that he was right, but not back then. I thought him to be extremely unreasonable. We were stubbornly unwilling to dissolve the friendship we had built. In a desperate attempt to get me out of his wife's life, Terri's husband hacked into my computer and sent emails to everyone in my address book telling them the whole sordid story. My mother, my children, my friends, and my pastor, each got an email exposing my sin. Words cannot begin to express my humiliation, my guilt. I was mortified. This was far worse for me than even when my husband had left. This was my sin, my choice, my affair. The control was in my hands, but my hands faltered and I fell from grace. I was so ashamed. The consequences of sin…more than you ever thought possible.

Feelings of absolute violation poured over me. I had even considered pressing charges against this man as he had used his work computer to hack into mine, and I knew his employer would have had a major problem. Instead, I was able, through prayer and the ministry of the Spirit, to step back and look at it from his point of view. For a brief moment, I walked in his shoes and realized that maintaining the friendship with his wife was wrong in every aspect—biblically and morally. After receiving some solid Christian counseling, I sat down with my dear friend and explained to her that we had to sever our friendship. It was heart-wrenching, but it was the right thing to do.

Terri had a difficult time accepting this, but I stood firm. Her husband's tactics were cruel but understandable. Nonetheless, he accomplished what he wanted—our friendship came to an end. Over the years, Terri has tried many times to continue to maintain contact. I knew I had to be the strong one and to keep the boundary—and I have now, for well over a decade.

Although some may look at Terri as the culprit in all of this because she was the "seasoned" Christian at the time and should have known better, I don't blame her at all for the breakdown in boundaries. It was just as much my fault as it was hers, and it was never planned. I was needy and she was unhappy in her marriage. We were both weak, so it happened. We both knew Christ; we both knew it was sin. It was a matter of making the wrong choice—together.

Terri's church, where I was attending at the time, made several attempts to walk along side me and address our relationship. They were insistent that we break off all contact, but we weren't willing to comply (something I now see as wise counsel). Since she was a member of the church, they enacted church discipline and eventually, due to her refusal to comply, asked her to leave the church. As a brand new believer, I was appalled at this and didn't understand their reaction or punishment. I now know that it was absolutely biblical. There is often a huge price for sin, and we were both paying for it dearly. During this time, I saw several counselors at the church who were very tough on me. I'm amazed that I continued in the faith after some of these "helping" interventions.

In regard to my family after they learned of my affair, passive indifference would best describe it. Remember, I was in the midst of a horrible, unexpected divorce. When I came to my "saving faith" in Christ and accepted Him as my Savior, my atheist brother said, "I know you were saved by Jesus," which nearly floored me. He was the last person I would expect to make that statement.

Most of my family was just so glad that I was eating again and looking better, that they didn't much care how it happened. They said very little about my relationship with Terri other than, "If you need help, we will do whatever we can to help you."

Becoming a Christian was a much bigger and much more disturbing thing to my family than the homosexual relationship. My daughter, who was in college at the time, was irritated at being bothered during her finals with the notice from Terri's husband. She was also irritated with me at how emotional I was over her father's affair. She thought that if someone was unhappy in the marriage it made perfect sense for them to move on. She was very hard-hearted toward my depression and thoroughly annoyed at my anorexia. She wanted me to "get up and get over it."

My middle son, Jesse, felt totally responsible for the whole ugly mess. He had been the one who told me that his father had a woman to the house while I was away with the other two children. As soon as he mentioned that this woman had been over, I knew there was trouble brewing and something wasn't right. Jesse was 11 at the time and he thought he had caused the divorce.

Jordan, my youngest, was only nine and a very contemplative boy. He became even more so, and when a local church began to minister to us he joined a Bible study and gave his life to Jesus. Only our Savior can make beauty out of ashes.

The healing was long coming. Again I spent many days and weeks in the dreariness of my darkened bedroom. I prayed constantly, but nothing seemed to penetrate the guilt I carried. My heart had grown cold and seemed to have crusted over in regrets. I reached out to a Christian recovery center and sought their help. I was still humiliated and in great need of advice and direction.

At first, I would get angry when anyone spoke of the joy of the Lord, for I had none. To tell you the truth, I was often blinded with thoughts of ending my life because of the pain—it ran so deep. I was pressed down by so much guilt and shame. I knew that dying had to be better than this life I was living.

The second night I was there I heard a sermon that "took me down". This man got up and spoke about trees and stumps. The crux was either that you are a tree—growing, flourishing, and bearing fruit for the Lord. Or you are a stump—dead and non-productive. Even more, you're in the way. Stumps are impediments—things to go around or trip over. I began to sob hysterically when I came to the realization of which one I was—a stump. I was no longer growing and flourishing for the Lord but becoming a dead thing; broken down by guilt and shame and self-loathing—unable to receive forgiveness or love from Christ—and I was in His way!

With little thought of me and all my focus now on Jesus, I went to my knees right there in that recovery center at the altar. I cried out to God, "Father, forgive me, restore me, and give me Your peace." I literally had to be peeled away from the altar to which I clung so desperately. It was as if I was melted into it, and so very broken before the Lord. Psalm 3:4 says, "I cried aloud to the Lord, and he answered me from his holy hill." Christ was calling my name.

Since I didn't know anyone at the recovery center and I was alone, I thought I would search out a place where there would be other women. The next day I returned and, even though I didn't sew, I joined a quilting class. I was so filled with shame that I couldn't look any of those women in the eyes. It was obvious that I was in distress. I was so afraid to mention my homosexuality. I thought for sure they would want nothing to do with me—but it was just the opposite. They surrounded me with love and support and followed the biblical teachings in Ephesians 2:4-6 "But God, being rich in mercy, because of the great love with which he loved us, even when we were dead in our trespasses, made us alive together with Christ–by grace you have been saved–and raised us up with him and seated us with him in the heavenly places in Christ Jesus." I was amazed, but God was just getting started.

Later that night, I listened to another man who gave his testimony of how Christ redeemed him from a life of drugs, alcohol, homosexuality and deep depravity. I knew God had put him there that night just for me. I felt as if God Himself had reached down through this man to minister healing into my crushed and broken spirit. At the end of the evening, I ran up to him in tears and thanked him for his words that I so desperately needed to hear—words of hope and understanding that I could be lifted up out of the darkness I felt.

This godly man spent many hours that week ministering comfort to me. It was the start of a very special friendship for which I thank God daily. 2Corinthians 1:3-5 says, "Blessed be the God and Father of our Lord Jesus Christ, the Father of mercies and God of all comfort, who comforts us in all our affliction, so that we may be able to comfort those who are in any affliction, with the comfort which we ourselves are comforted by God. For as we share abundantly in Christ's sufferings, so through Christ we share abundantly in comfort too."

Today I stand here as a living testimony to the love and grace of Jesus Christ and His healing power. I am filled with unimaginable joy and the desire to serve Christ as He leads me wherever He needs me. I am no longer broken. My life is full and my heart is overflowing. I am a work in progress, a sinner saved by grace, covered by the blood and redeemed in love.

Psalm 30:11-12, "You have turned for me my mourning into dancing; you have loosed my sackcloth and clothed me with gladness, that my glory may sing your praise and not be silent. Oh Lord, my God, I will give thanks to you forever. Psalm 31:1, "In you, O Lord, I do take refuge; let me never be put to shame; deliver me in your righteousness."

Terri and I had a 15-year friendship. She was a dear, caring, loving, giving friend with whom the boundaries were crossed. We never meant for it to happen. And while I don't consider myself a lesbian, I have always had an attraction to women. I was drawn to them; I admired their beauty and grace; and I saw things in them that I did not have. I never thought about the intimacy part before, or if I did, I quickly dismissed it knowing it was wrong. This was the first and only actual homosexual relationship I ever had.

It would be easy for me to be in a same sex relationship/

marriage, and I think I would be happy, but not if it is, as the Bible clearly states, a sin. So I have learned to be content as a single woman. Not pursuing a homosexual lifestyle is a sacrifice that I have made to my Lord Jesus out of love and obedience to Him and to His word. It is my love offering. I have several very close male friendships and they are very dear to me. I miss having someone intimately in my life, but for now God has me single and I believe this is best.

Out of all the years Terri and I were friends, only five of those years were spent in sexual behavior. Not that this minimizes our sin, it's just a fact. The rest of the time was a beautiful friendship, although quite enmeshed.

Soon I was directed to counseling at a place called Harvest in Philadelphia, a ministry for same sex attracted people. For the year that I was there, I received amazing counseling and at no cost. I also had the privilege of writing my testimony for one of their publications and to share my testimony at a conference there for counselors and therapists who work with same sex attracted clients. What an incredible thing that was, to see God using my worst sin for His glory—and He continues to do so today.

Through mutual friends, I heard that Terri and her husband were, over time, able to reconcile. Knowing that they came through this storm together gives me a great sense of peace and happiness. I also learned that their family has grown and they are now grandparents. I am overjoyed by this news and continue to pray for them all.

My identity is not derived from my sexual preferences,

behaviors, or temptations, but from my right standing with God through faith in Jesus as my Lord and Savior. I consider myself a beloved child of God.

This year I will be starting my 20th year as an elementary teacher for the 3rd and 4th graders in the Upper Perkiomen School District in Pennsylvania. When I retire in a few years, I would like to serve in a place where I can use the gifts God has given me and my testimony to help others come to the saving grace of our Savior, Jesus Christ. Until then, I know that I am forgiven. I am redeemed. I have been made new. I no longer feel the shame of what my life used to be. That was another time. This is now. God has filled me with hope. My story is His glory and I will shout it to the world.

Closing Thoughts:

This book is a work of God at His best and I am humbled and honored that He has used me to help tell these stories you have just read—true stories of ordinary people going through extraordinary challenges and putting all their faith into Someone much bigger and stronger—Someone who promises to "never leave you nor forsake you," (Hebrews 13:5)—no matter what this life brings. These people know that, even though they have gone through hell in this life, they will one day be in Heaven with their Savior for all eternity.

Unfortunately, there are still those people who believe that they can get into Heaven just by being a good person. This is a misconception by so many who think that, as long as they treat people decently (like helping others or giving to charities), and don't do anything too horrible (like cheat, steal, or kill), that they, too, will be allowed through Heaven's gate. But, it is clearly stated in the Bible that it is "...by grace you have been saved through faith...it is a gift of God, not of works, lest anyone should boast" (Ephesians 2:8-9). In other words, you cannot get to Heaven by the things you do here on earth! The Bible calls it "works"—and no amount of "works" is good enough to get in.

There is only one way into Heaven and that is through Jesus Christ—God's only begotten Son. Jesus said in John 14:6, "I am the way, the truth, and the life. No one comes to the Father except through Me" (bold print mine). God promises if we believe in Jesus—that He died for us on the cross and rose again and we repent of our sins—that we will live in Heaven for all eternity with Him. And with the only other option being Hell, why would anyone not want to follow Christ—even if their struggles and hardships in this life are much more difficult or challenging, or even (at times) too painful to bear? The Light at the end of it all is well worth anything we would have to go through without Him. Plus, we get the honor and privilege of serving our Creator and bringing Him the glory He deserves while we are still part of this world. "Give to the Lord the glory due His name" (Psalm 96:8).

With Christ comes the greatest hope and He helps us to endure the hard times by giving us patience. "My brethren, count it all joy when you fall into various trials, knowing that the testing of your faith produces patience" (James 1:2-3). However, when we choose to follow the Lord, we also become targets for Satan and it is only a matter of time before his evil attacks turn into "spiritual warfare". When this happens, it is important for us to be armed with God's strength so that we can fight back—and this type of strength comes from persecution. "Yes and all who desire to live godly in Christ Jesus will suffer persecution" (2Timothy 3:12). But the "Good" news is, God will never tempt or give us beyond what we can do. "No temptation has overtaken you except such as is common to man; but God is faithful, who will not allow you to be tempted beyond what you are able, but with the temptation will also make the way for escape, that you may be able to bear it" (1Corinthians 10:13).

We can also take comfort knowing that no misfortune or tragedy can come to us that the Father does not allow. Satan is so held by the Almighty God that he can only strike where and when he is given permission (Job 1:12). God who has "shut in the sea with doors" and said, "This far you may come, but no farther; and here your proud waves must stop!" (Job 38:8, 11) will keep Satan under His command and not allow him to do anything that He does not first approve.

God always knows what we are going through and, on top of that, He allows it to happen. So, you can be sure He must have a good reason for it! "And we know that all things work together for good to those who love God, to those who are the called according to His purpose" (Romans 8:28).

God will use our trials and troubles to make us stronger which, in turn, makes us more dependent on Him so He can use us for His purpose. Our trials also provide us the opportunity to help others, especially for those who are going through similar circumstances. "Praise be to God and the Father of our Lord Jesus Christ, the Father of compassion and the God of all comfort, who comforts us in all our troubles so that we can comfort those in any trouble with the comfort we ourselves have received from God" (2Corinthians 1:3-4). What better witness is there than someone who has already suffered what we ourselves are going through? That is what "Dancing with the Scars" is all about!

I am so proud of all the brave people in this book who stepped up in their God-given faith to relive their difficult stories and then share them with all of you. And even though some may feel the sting of embarrassment by what they went through because of the choices they made, they know that telling their story will bring glory to God, for it was He who kept them strong and helped them through their darkest hour.

These precious people might be slightly damaged from all they had to go through in this life, but you can be sure they will be "dancing with their scars"—from this day forward—into eternity.

For All My Readers

To Know Him Is To Love Him

If any of the stories in this book have stirred your heart in the slightest, you can be sure it is God and He is talking to you! If you do not know His Son, Jesus Christ, as your personal Savior, please take a few minutes to read the following paragraphs. They will show you how to surrender your life fully to Jesus and become a child of God. Remember, there isn't anything you've done that God won't forgive nor is there anything you can't get through if God is in your heart—and you let the Holy Spirit guide your every step. Succumb to Him. I promise it will be worth it—then let Him have the first dance—scars and all...

How Do I Become a Christian?

John 3:1-3 Now there was a man of the Pharisees, named Nicodemus, a ruler of the Jews; this man came to Jesus by night and said to Him, "Rabbi, we know that You have come from God as a teacher; for no one can do these signs that You do unless God is with him." Jesus answered and said to him, "Truly, truly, I say to you, unless one is born again he cannot see the kingdom of God."

Jesus was teaching that, since all men are born with a sin nature, we are born spiritually dead to the "things" of God. It takes the Holy Spirit of God working in us to bring us spiritually alive to God. This is called "being born again." As the Holy Spirit calls those whom God has chosen, the question frequently asked is, "What must I do to be saved?"

Luke recorded an event in Acts 16:22-34 where this question was asked. The Apostle Paul was imprisoned, along with Silas, when a great earthquake occurred and the doors were opened and their chains released. The jailer became very frightened since he would be held accountable for losing his prisoners. When he saw that Paul and Silas were still there, he asked the question, "Sirs, what must I do to be saved?" They said, "Believe in the Lord Jesus, and you will be saved, you and your household" (Acts 16:30-31).

In those days, when the head of the household became saved, the rest of his family usually followed his leadership. Throughout the Bible, the requirement for salvation is faith.

One might ask, "Faith in what?" Our faith must be in the fact that Jesus Christ is Lord, meaning God. He came to us in the form of a man, born of the Virgin Mary, for the sole purpose of shedding His blood on the cross, a perfect sacrifice for paying the penalty for our sins. And our faith must include our belief in His resurrection; the fact that He rose from the dead on the third day and He is alive forevermore in heaven. There are those who are of the opinion that there are many ways to God; that it is not necessary to believe in Jesus, but that is not what God's word says. One of the attributes of God is that He cannot lie. Let us read two verses in Scripture:

(Acts 4:12) "And there is salvation in no one else; for there is no other name under heaven that has been given among men by which we must be saved."

(John 14:5) Jesus said to him, "I am the way, and the truth, and the life; no one comes to the Father but through Me."

Standing Guilt-free Before God?

(2Corinthians 7:10) For the sorrow that is according to the will of God produces repentance without regret, leading to salvation, but the sorrow of the world produces death.

Repentance means that I have seen myself as God sees me, that I recognize my evil deeds and the goodness of God. When I begin to see my own wickedness against the background of God's holiness; His perfect goodness, love, and righteousness, I am led to what the Bible calls a

"Godly sorrow." This means that I am not just sorry for getting caught in sin, but that I have a true, great remorse for my sinful condition; that I truly seek God's forgiveness and commit to change my evil ways…to turn around and follow God's ways rather than my own, independent ways. It means that I will no longer seek approval from the world, but commit to live to serve and please God.

When we repent and receive Jesus Christ as our Lord and Savior, we are completely forgiven of all our sins. We are cleansed. Our sins are removed and transferred to the sacrifice of Jesus. All our sins were laid upon Him. Since our sins are cleansed away by God, all our guilt is also removed. We stand before God blameless. Because of God's mercy and grace upon our lives, we are also to forgive others in the same manner that He has forgiven us; this we must be willing to do in order to reflect the love of God to others who are in need of the same forgiveness that we have just received from God. Now we are free. We are free of sin, guilt, and the bitterness of hating others who have offended us. We are free to experience the joy of God's love and forgiveness; free to serve Him, free to love others, free to receive God's promise of eternal life in His heaven, and free to do our part in building His kingdom.

(John 3:16) "For God so loved the world that He gave His only begotten Son, that whoever believes in Him shall not perish, but have eternal life."

Saved from God's Judgment?

One might ask the question, "How can I know that I am a sinner?" We can find the answer to that question in God's word. (Romans 3:23) For all have sinned and fall short of the glory of God, and in (Romans 6:23) For the wages of sin is death, but the free gift of God is eternal life in Christ Jesus our Lord.

Because of God's righteousness and justice, each and every sin requires the penalty of death. Even Adam's "original sin nature" is transferred to us, therefore without Jesus Christ, we stand condemned. But because of God's love and mercy, we are saved through the sacrifice of Jesus Christ who died on our behalf so that we (everyone who believes) can be forgiven. Salvation means that we are saved from God's wrath.

Is Jesus Real?

(Luke 1:46-47) And Mary said; "My soul exalts the Lord, and my spirit has rejoiced in God my Savior."

Is Jesus very real to us? We cannot see Him, hear Him, or touch Him. We have the Scriptures to rely on and the faith God has given us. But is He real? When the Christ child leaped into Mary's womb He became very real! Her soul soared and she rejoiced. Her emotions were very real. She knew He was present and, before He was born, she knew He was our Savior and she acknowledges her own need of a savior. Jesus is not someone that is part of our lives sometimes. He must be real. He must not be just part of our lives, but the focus of our lives; the purpose of our lives. He is the One we will spend eternity with. Like Mary, the mother of Jesus, let us rejoice in Him every day.

Christians know that this life isn't always easy but they are confident and reassured in Christ and by Christ that one day when this life has passed, that they will be in a place like no other...laughing, loving, and living once again...a place where love abides and God is at our side for all eternity.

(Psalm 62:6) He only is my rock and my salvation; He is my defense; I shall not be moved.

All the amazing individuals in this book have the same reasons for writing their stories. And that is to help someone else through whatever pain, struggle, trial, or test of faith they are going through or have already gone through. We're in this together, coming together for the soul purpose in bringing our Savior the glory He deserves. May you know Him and serve Him with joy and delight forever.

Obeying His Call!

(Isaiah 6:8) Then I heard the voice of the Lord, saying, "Whom shall I send, and who will go for us?'" Then I said, "Here am I. Send me!"

There is no higher calling, no greater privilege, than that of being called by God to accomplish some small part of His plan. God does not call us to do easy tasks. He calls us to do the impossible and we cannot possibly do what He calls us to do unless we rely completely on Him.

Every believer in Christ has a purpose; a calling to some particular ministry—prayer, faith, planning, courage, and perseverance are the essentials for successful ministry—there is no greater blessing than seeing God working through us in bringing truth and help to those who are thirsty and in need of the knowledge of God. When Isaiah saw the Majesty of God—when he saw His power and His glory—when he experienced His love and His mercy, his only response was, "Yes, send me!"

Also Available from TJ Martini

Joe's Bible
A Teen's Journey to Salvation

On December 15, 2001, brothers Dan and Joe Scafidi were driving home after a day on the ski slopes and inadvertently drifted off the side of the road, killing them both instantly. This is the true story of a young girl named Ashley, who desperately seeks to find answers after the untimely death of her best friend and his brother and how her journey eventually leads her to a peace she has never known before.

Blue Side Up
An Angel Among Us

The true story of the ill-fated Alaska Airlines Flight 261 when it spiraled out of control and plunged into the dark waters of the Pacific Ocean, on January 31, 2000, and of a remarkable flight attendant, Kristin Mills, who was faced with the most important decision of her life.

Standing on the Edge of Eternity

The fictitious story of five individuals whose lives will simultaneously come to a tragic end on the first Sunday after Christmas. Although they all die in different ways and never know one another, all five must face the consequences of their earthly decisions as they enter into the only common ground they have between them: Eternity! Do you know where you will be spending yours?

I Never Thought I Would Beg My Husband To Go To A Strip Club

This sad but true story is based on the life of a little girl lost, in a world where she does not belong; a world of sex, prostitution, drugs, pornography, and strip clubs, and a mother on a mission to save her precious child. Walk with her through every raunchy hell-hole in her daughter's pathetic life as she lives this nightmare that never seems to end.

Even If

The Story of Reverend George Mayes, Jr.

Walk by faith, not by sight. George Mayes Jr. learned this lesson the hard way when a debilitating eye disease turned his world into total darkness, sending him down a road he never dreamed he'd have to walk.

Dancing With The Scars

True Stories of Hope Restored

This book centers on nearly two dozen true stories of ordinary but very real people from all over the globe who share the most extraordinary challenges of their lives; how they made it through and how they survived. Although the challenges and heartaches these people suffered are not what we normally experience in life, these survivors hope that their stories will help people everywhere who are going through difficult times or painful circumstances. They want you to know and believe that there is hope for you and that you are not alone! This book will show you that there isn't anything you can't get through in this life if you are willing to put your trust where it matters most, in the loving arms of God.

For information about TJ Martini, or to book her for speaking engagements, please visit: www.tjmartini.com

CPSIA information can be obtained
at www.ICGtesting.com
Printed in the USA
FSOW02n1650300816
24398FS